Thank you!
Suzanne Reuben

Not Gone With The Wind

Not Gone With The Wind

The three stories of Hurricane Harvey
Rockport, Fulton, and Aransas County, Texas
Landfall on August 25, 2017

by Suzanne Reuber

Copyright © 2018 Suzanne Reuber

All rights reserved. This book is protected by copyright. No part of it may be reproduced, stored in a retrieval system, or transmitted in any form or by any means, elctronic, mechanical, photocopying, recording, or otherwise, without the prior permission of the publisher.

Picture Credits: Suzanne Reuber, Nancy Paulson, NOAA Hurricane Harvey Report at https://www.weather.gov/crp/hurricane_harvey

Published by Classworks Publishing

ISBN: 1-7326363-1-1
ISBN-13: 978-1-7326363-1-6

DEDICATION

The harbor was filled with boat carcasses; the aquarium was flattened; the Rockport Center for the Arts was severely damaged; the Pavilions on the beach were unusable. Their neighbor, The Woman's Club of Aransas County, had minor damage; the building was NOT gone with the wind. The Woman's Club became home to SBA on September 3 and then to FEMA operations for six weeks after Harvey. It is still providing space for groups whose meeting places are unusable. This book is dedicated to the Woman's Club on its 70th birthday and to its members who through those years have worked diligently to allow the club to continue to serve the community.

Woman's Club of Aransas County
Before and after Harvey

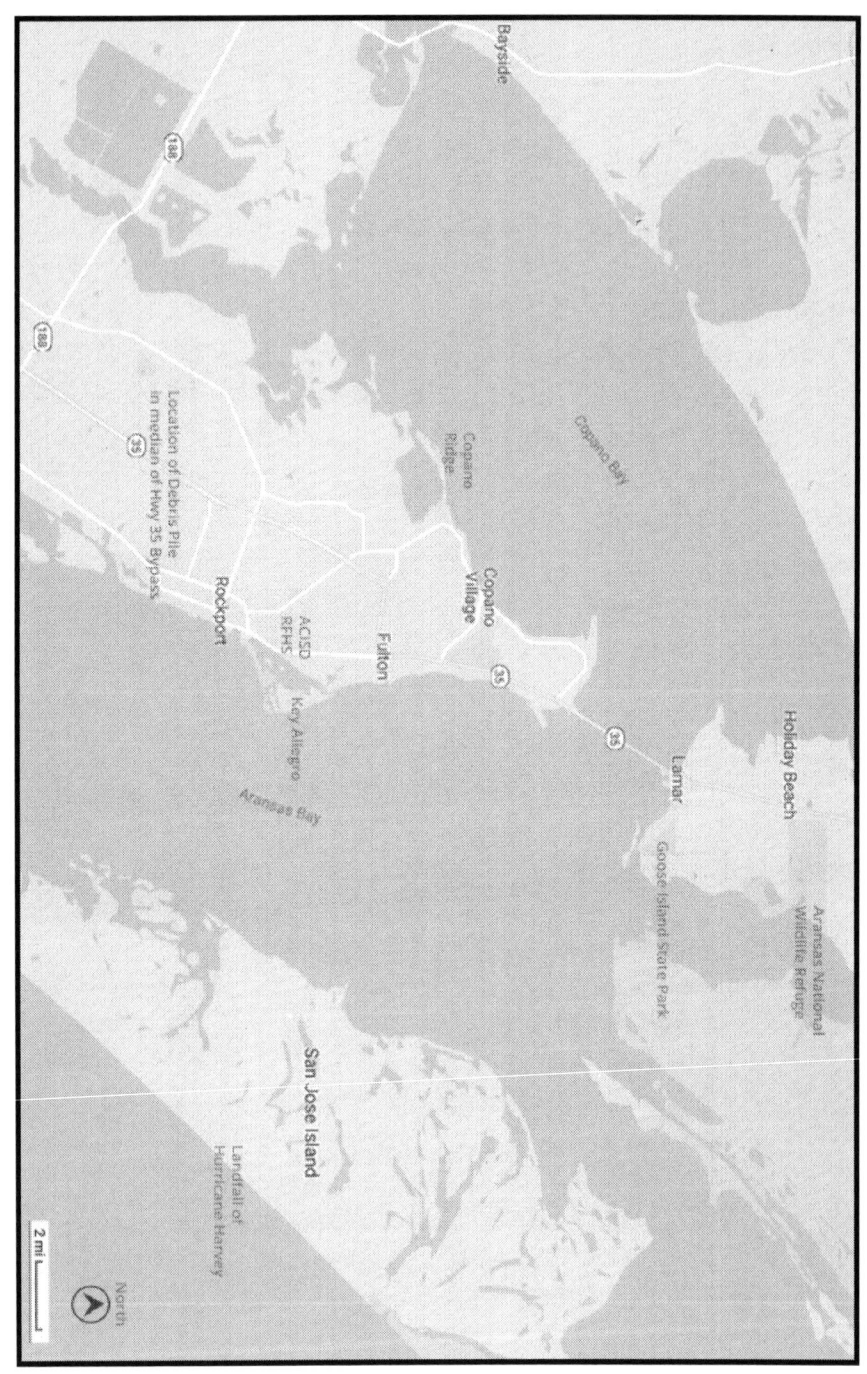

TABLE OF CONTENTS

FOREWORD XIII
PREFACE XV
BEFORE HARVEY: NORMAL 1
   June 1, 2017 Thursday 1
   August 1, 2017 Tuesday 2
   August 10, 2017 Wednesday 4
   August 20, 2017 Sunday 5
   August 21, 2017 Monday 6
TRANSITIONS 7
   Why visit Rockport-Fulton-Lamar? 7
   Why Stay Longer in Rockport-Fulton-Lamar? 9
   Why Live in Rockport-Fulton-Lamar? 13
HURRICANES 15
BEFORE HARVEY: FRANTIC 17
   August 22, 2017 Tuesday 17
   August 23, 2017 Wednesday, 10:15 am 18
   August 23, 2017 Wednesday, 4:15 pm 19
   August 23, 2017 Wednesday, 10:15 pm 20
   August 24, 2017 Thursday, 4:15 am 21
   August 24, 2017 Thursday, 10:15 am 21
DURING HARVEY: SURVIVAL 33
   August 25, 2017 Friday afternoon 33
   August 25-26, 2017 Friday night-Saturday morning 38
THE AFTERMATH: DISASTER 53
   August 26-August 28, 2017 Saturday-Monday 53
   EARLY RESPONDERS 59
   August 28 - September 9, 2017, ... 63
   COPANO BAY AND KEY ALLEGRO 87
   COORDINATION 95
   CHURCHES 99
THE AFTERMATH: POWER 103
   September 10-October 11, 2017 103
   THE KINDNESS OF STRANGERS 124
   INDEPENDENCE 133
   ANIMALS 137
THE AFTERMATH: THE NEW NORMAL 143
   October 12-December 10, 2017 143
   HARVEY'S TOLL AS OF DECEMBER, 2017: 149
   TREES 151
   In Conclusion 155
ACKNOWLEDGMENTS 157

FOREWORD

As a small contributor to this book, it was an honor and a privilege to meet the author. To have someone approach you with a sincere and dedicated focus to document the events and stories of those who experienced Hurricane Harvey first-hand was so timely and so needed. Having read the finished product, I can say that whether it is just one year or twenty years from now a new reader wondering what it was like will come away with a true sense of what the citizens of Aransas County endured before, during and shortly after August 25, 2017. Suzy Reuber, thank you for gathering the facts, interviewing countless folks, putting it in print, telling the story and personal accounts of when a historic Cat 4 hurricane ravaged our community.

Rick McLester

Emergency Management Coordinator

Aransas County, City of Rockport, Town of Fulton

PREFACE

Chainsaw skills ... non-existent. Banned from ladders after unfortunate experience. Allergic to mold. Stamina ... limited. I wanted to help but my skill set was a bit of a barrier. I spent most of a fifty-year career in education listening to stories. Some were possible and even plausible. Most were neither. But the stories were part of the background of the person telling them, and as such, were very real. Not great preparation for helping after a hurricane.

Arriving in Rockport in December, I was appalled, especially after hearing how much better it looked now than it did three months ago. On impulse, I said to my friend Mary Anne ... "tell me your hurricane story." Two hours later, I had found a job. I could listen to people tell me about Harvey. I thought that many people would not want to talk about Harvey and would turn down my request. I was so wrong. Over 100 interviews later, I had never been turned down. I had talked to a Mayor, a hairdresser, a veterinarian, a firefighter, a birder, a waitress, several church leaders, multiple volunteers, a school superintendent, a principal, the emergency management coordinator, briefly a governor, a librarian, many Winter Texans, many Rockport residents, a catfish whisperer, a real estate agent, a chiropractor, an optometrist and many people who had not evacuated, despite the mandatory order.

Some stories were uplifting, others heartbreaking, and

others hysterically funny. Most of all, the stories are very personal. I knew that these stories needed to be preserved.

Depending on the story teller, there are at least three Harvey hurricanes. Winter Texans saw Harvey in technicolor and their stories reflect the brilliant reds and oranges they saw on their television. Those who evacuated and returned often talk about Harvey in shades of grey ... Weather Channel pictures of slashing rain and winds, dead trees, piles of debris. Those who did not evacuate tell stories that are very black generally followed by "I will never stay during a hurricane again." Only they had first hand experience of what it is like to survive a direct hit by a Category 4 hurricane. Only when the three sets of stories are combined do you get a full picture of Harvey. The stories paint Harvey's portrait.

Maybe I could write a book.

Pre-Harvey Downtown Rockport

BEFORE HARVEY: Normal

June 1, 2017 Thursday

Aransas County, Texas

Once a year during the summer, we would meet with our school district insurer, Regional Pool Alliance, and their disaster recovery organization, North Star Recovery. We would update our records, pass on new phone numbers, possibly look at any changes in our physical plant, shake hands and say "See you next year." Once a year, that was it for 15 years.

Pre-Harvey Lighthouse Inn

Not Gone With The Wind

First day of Hurricane Season. It happens every year; who cared? Fortunately, lots of people pay attention. The Aransas County Emergency Operations Center (EOC) would, in the case of a declared emergency, begin meeting four times a day, at 10 am, 4 pm, 10pm, and 4 am until the emergency was over. The 10-4 trucker CB response for "I understand" may not be a coincidence. All 74 participants knew the drill. All was calm. Except for the tourists, of course. But, that is a "known" type of craziness.

August 1, 2017 Tuesday

Texas

Texas is huge and often has huge disasters. As a result, most government agencies are required to have disaster plans in place at all levels to cover all the most common disasters. Chemical plant explosions? Check. Hurricanes? Check. Fires? Check. Blizzards, ice storms, tornados? Check. Meetings and trainings are held at all levels. Procedures? Check. Personnel? Check. Materials? Check. August 1, 2017 is just another day; Texas is ready.

American Electric Power

AEP plans ahead. Staging areas for every foreseeable disaster are contracted for a year in advance. Materials are in place in or near the staging areas. The network of companies in the AEP group are ready to send disaster crews on short notice. Electrical workers are always prepared to send help to affected areas. August 1, 2017 is just another day; AEP is ready.

Aransas County, TX

EOC meetings are often as exciting as any business staff meetings. I go but often think...already another meeting? I have places to be, people to talk to. I wonder if this meeting will be worth the time. I also know that my seat better be occupied or I will regret it.

Aransas County is the second smallest county in Texas; located between Corpus Christi and Houston, the permanent population, including the "urban" areas

Pre-Harvey First Presbyterian Church

of Rockport-Fulton-Lamar, is no more than 25,000. The area of Aransas County is 528 square miles and half of that is under water. Meetings and trainings are held regularly in the Emergency Operations Center (EOC) that involve representatives of all organizations and people of the communities that could be impacted by a disaster. Preparations have to include both land and water disasters. It is hurricane season but August 1, 2017 is just another day; Aransas County is ready.

In charge of disaster coordination at the local level is an Emergency Management Coordinator; in the case of Aransas County-Rockport-Fulton-Lamar, Rick McLester wears this hat along with that of Fulton Police Chief and several others. The emergency plans are in place, dating from many years ago and regularly updated. The department heads or supervisors of all the major programs in the area, meet at the Emergency Operations Center in downtown Rockport to get the information they need to carry out their emergency plans. This group of approximately 75 people includes local government entities, school superintendent, nursing facility coordinators, business owners, church leaders…all local, all know a certain segment of the community. When a hurricane threatens, the meetings are frequent, at 10 am, 4 pm, 10 pm, and 4 am, tied into a conference call from John Metz, meteorologist, with National Weather Service. Often, the hurricane doesn't really develop or impact Aransas County. Doesn't matter. Attendance at the meetings is compulsory.

Rockport-Fulton, TX

The urban areas of Aransas County have a varying population, no more than 12,000 permanent residents. However, when the summer tourists and the Winter Texans come to town, the population may double. Permanent residents may know procedures (and ignore them); tourists are often not aware of possible danger. Officials know this and prepare accordingly. August 1, 2017 is just another day; Rockport and Fulton are ready.

August 10, 2017 Wednesday

Aransas County Independent School District

I can hardly wait to get back in my room. I am going to change out the bulletin boards, check out the new materials, look over my class list…I am ready for summer in May but I am really ready for school to start in August! Just as the kids miss their friends, teachers miss their friends too.

I like my school and I am going to have the teacher that I wanted! She is so nice. Two of my friends are in my class, I think. Summer has gotten kind of boring ... I am ready for school.

We should have a good volleyball team this year. Every year is different but I think that our team will be a surprise for everyone.

Teachers are back for the first day of preparations for the 2017-2018 school year. It is an exciting time for school personnel. Disaster plans have more urgency, given the number of school shootings, and procedures are reviewed. Hurricane disaster plans have been in place for many years and are updated yearly. School enrollment is around 3400 students. The football team and volleyball team have been practicing for the opening game. August 9, 2017 is a great day; ACISD is ready for a new school year.

Pre-Harvey Zachary Taylor Park Gazebo

August 20, 2017 Sunday

Aransas County/Rockport/Fulton/Lamar

We are Winter Texans in an RV park and decided last year to leave our 5th wheel on site rather than pulling it to Sinton....for the first time. What could go wrong?

Sunday before Harvey, we wondered if we had made the right decision. Maybe we should drive down from Nebraska and pull the trailer to Sinton. It was hurricane season, after all. That 5th wheel held my memories. But the eclipse distracted us.

Nothing out of the ordinary. Business as usual. HEB and Walmart are busy. Churches are full. Restaurants are packed. The RV parks are still full of summer tourists. First Responders in Aransas County are always ready.

August 21, 2017 Monday

Aransas County Independent School District

My room is ready. I know just what I am going to do... at least for the first three or four days. After I get to know the kids, my plans will change. They always do. So exciting!

I get to ride a bus this year with my friend. I think mom is ready for school to start. She has all my stuff right by the front door.

First day of school! Teachers' classrooms are ready. Lunches are ready. Staff is ready. Football and volleyball players are ready. ACISD is ready. It is going to be a great school year!

Pre-Harvey Rockport Aquarium

TRANSITIONS

Why visit Rockport-Fulton-Lamar?

As a Winter Texan from Kansas, the "why" seems obvious; ice, sleet and snow are powerful motivators. The "where" is generational; my parents wintered in Rockport and I drove them down. More fool me, I then flew home to ice, sleet and snow.

I am a Winter Texan from Michigan and now a resident of Rockport. We started out in Circle W RV Park in 1995 and stayed there for 10 years; then we bought a house in in Rockport in 2005. I don't miss Michigan in January and February.

We lived in Illinois and wintered in Rockport. Winter ... it was an obvious decision. Summer...I can be hot and uncomfortable in Texas just as easy as in Illinois. We kept staying later and later every year.

Not Gone With The Wind

Rockport is an unlikely site for a dream vacation. White sandy beaches? No. Consistently blue-green placid water? No. Casinos and night clubs that will accommodate thousands? No. The derivation of the name, Aransas, is said to come from a word meaning "thorny". Rattlesnakes outnumber people by a wide margin. However, mention Rockport in many parts of Michigan, Illinois, Minnesota, Wisconsin, North and South Dakota, Nebraska, Kansas and Oklahoma and the recognition is instant. "We have wintered there for years!" The population almost doubles between October and March. Rockport has an active winter fan club.

Winter Texans come for many of the same reasons that permanent residents of Rockport stay. The local residents are welcoming, especially since many of them came to get away from winter cold also. Churches are abundant and look forward to their winter congregation's arrival. The RV and trailer parks fill up and the potluck meals outside become regular events ... in January.

Volunteering is common among the Winter Texans. The docents in the Fulton Mansion ... probably from Minnesota since they talk funny. Sorting clothes at the Castaways thrift shop ... could be from anywhere. History Center guides ... likewise. Rockport Center for the Arts ... artists from all over come to the area. Woman's Club of Aransas County ... winter bridge/canasta/mahjong players support scholarships in Aransas County and the library. Most Winter Texans were busy in their hometown and just transfer their energy to their winter home town.

A dream vacation spent on the beach? Maybe not. A chance to know and be known in a town that welcomes transplants? Definitely.

Why Stay Longer in Rockport-Fulton-Lamar?

We spend six months a year in Canada and six months in Rockport, a best of both worlds marriage. Our 5th wheel trailer stays in Canada; our Park Model trailer is in Rockport. We have best friends here and when we drive through the gates of our park, we know we are home.

We visited Rockport one winter and bought our Park Model before we left for Michigan. We made the decision faster than most but we also came from a place that is colder than most. That was fifteen years ago. Still living in the same Park Model.

Pre-Harvey Compass Rose Park in Rockport

Not Gone With The Wind

Rockport started with aspirations. Early founders dreamed of a major city with a railroad connecting it to the big cities and a large port with ship building facilities. Without dreamers, progress stalls; sometimes it stalls even with dreamers. A Civil War, multiple storms, politics ... the area adapted. Eventually, there was a railroad connecting the beef processing plants and sea food processing industries to the rest of the world. Ship building facilities developed, just at the end of WWI. But the 1919 hurricane dumped sand into Copano Bay, making it too shallow. The dream of a deep water port and a major city lost out to the city of Corpus Christi.

By then, Rockport had been discovered by various business titans ... not as a place to do business as much as a place for a second home. Sea breezes in Rockport made

Pre-Harvey Beachfront Pavilion at Rockport Beach Park

the climate more attractive in the summer than the heat of central Texas. Those same virtues of a tropical climate that made Rockport attractive to business titans also attracted northerners who decided that winter had lost its charms.

The Winter Texans, or Snow Birds as they were known for a while, didn't really want a second home. They wanted respite from winter. Tourist cabins and motels began to be built, tiny cramped little places with kitchenettes ... a euphemism for a closet with a sink and hot plate. And people came and stayed for three months ... and loved it. It was warm, mostly, and sunny, mostly, and the same people came back to the same places year after year. The fishing was excellent, particularly when the hook was baited, and the company of fellow fisherman was even better. The motels upgraded and added swimming pools, tiny but heated, and outdoor picnic tables. The non-fishing Winter Texans perfected happy hours ... 5:00 pm, rain or shine. Everyone was invited. The fishing piers were reinforced with rails and benches for sitting. Now the motels were full summer and winter; Rockport had become a tourist mecca.

An interesting pattern began to develop. The Winter Texans found it hard to leave, come the end of March. Some from the northern tier of states found themselves interested in weaving their way home by way of children and grandchildren, arriving back home with spring in late April and early May. They discovered the joys of mobile living. Some bought trailers, others bought RV's, allowing Winter Texans to visit grandkids without have to stay in the spare bedroom around the grumpy son-in-law. Entrepreneurs in Rockport began providing a place to park their rigs ... for a fee, of course. The trailer parks upgraded; tiny, but heated swimming pools, picnic tables under the live oaks,

Pre-Harvey Fulton Harbor

fishing piers. The mobile Winter Texans loved it and, pulling their rigs, returned year after year.

Eventually, mobility lost its charm for some. Enter the Park Model, a trailer that doesn't go anywhere. The owners traveled by car or truck from their chilly Northern home and could stay in their southern home as long as they wanted. Others bought a condo or built homes in Rockport and started arriving in October and leaving in April. Eventually, many of those Transitioning Texans settled in and were no longer tourists but Rockport residents. They live in Rockport because they love the town. And are envied by Winter Texans who can't leave behind their much loved northern homes.

Pre-Harvey Fulton Convention Center (Paws and Taws)

Why Live in Rockport-Fulton-Lamar?

I moved here with my new husband 16 years ago because Rockport was where he wanted to live and train dogs. I knew no one. I made many friends throughout the area through my church, the Woman's Club, and my horse. Rockport is my home.

After a career in the military, my husband announced that for retirement, he wanted big salt water. Rockport came to the top of the list, not even knowing about the top notch fishing. We moved in 2005 and I realized that I wasn't ready to retire. So I opened Rockport Web Sites. We were home.

I live in Rockport because I love it. I began visiting 40 years ago, moved here 30 years ago, and have lived in my house for 25 years. And I still sound like I live in New York. Go figure.

I was born in Texas, lived in Missouri for many years, and came back to Texas. The memories were better here. My mother came back also, shortly before Harvey. Timing is everything. No regrets.

I grew up in Rockport. As a teenager, I loved the band shell by the beach, the crab, the surfing. I remember the shell had the slogan "Rockport: the Toast of the Coast" with a picture of a martini glass. As with any teen, I couldn't wait to get out, see the world. Later, I couldn't wait to get back.

I'm a Texan who came to Rockport 30 some years ago because there was a job here. The job is still here and so am I. Rockport and I have bonded. This is home.

Not Gone With The Wind

Permanent residents live in Rockport for many of the same reasons that tourists come. It rarely snows, and when it does, someone will write a book about it. The fishing is great and fishing guides guard their best sites zealously. The beach is lovely ... and protected by the barrier island from the Gulf of Mexico. The seafood ... fish, oysters, shrimp, crabs ... is fresh, as in straight-off-the-boat fresh. No one is surprised to see a 90 year-old with a cane and binoculars on the birding trails in January. Locals accept the occasional traffic jam, allowing as how no one ever learned to back up in Wisconsin. They are appalled at the thought of living in the big cities of Houston and San Antonio but think nothing of whipping over to Houston for shopping. They complain about all the usual things ... politicians, potholes, building codes ... but refuse to consider living anywhere else.

Rockport Strong sign made for a survivor and becoming our slogan

HURRICANES

Weather has window stickers. So do cars. Car dealers have developed names for discriminating between similar things so that the observer can compare these similar things at a glance. For example, a subcompact seats 4 comfortably with 85 to 99 cubic feet of passenger and cargo volume. A compact seats 5 comfortably and has 100 to 109 cubic feet of passenger and cargo volume. The discriminating shopper can tell which car is which by the way they look; the window stickers then tell about features that are hidden. Then there are the brand names; Chevy, Honda, GMC are easily recognizable. Those brand names carry with them a lot of general information. The window sticker provides the detail.

Meteorologists have a time problem with their window stickers. The same storm may have multiple designations before it is finished. Tropical depression, tropical storm, hurricane or typhoon ... how best to help the observer know what they are seeing? And, how to keep their storms straight when the same kind of storms seem to be chasing each other across the same territory?

The Saffir-Simpson Hurricane Scale provides some help. Category 1: Wind Speed 74 to 95 mph; storm surge 4-5 feet; Damage minimal. Category 4: Wind Speed 131-155 mph; storm surge 13-18 feet; Damage extreme. Experienced hurricane participants sneer at a Category 1 Storm. Not so much at a Category 4.

So, thanks to Saffir-Simpson, hurricane categories exist with defining characteristics ... Category 1, Category 4 ... but not discriminating characteristics. The "if you have seen one Category 4 hurricane, you have seen them all" approach doesn't work well. So meteorologists, like car makers, discovered names ... brand names, if you will. Those names now carry data and images ... Katrina, for example. Certain rules exist for moving a numbered tropical depression to a named storm but once named, everything associated with that storm carries the name. It has been branded.

Unexpected, Harvey is about to be branded. Not only branded, but like many residents of Rockport, eventually retired. And Rockport, Fulton, and Aransas County will once again need to adapt to survive.

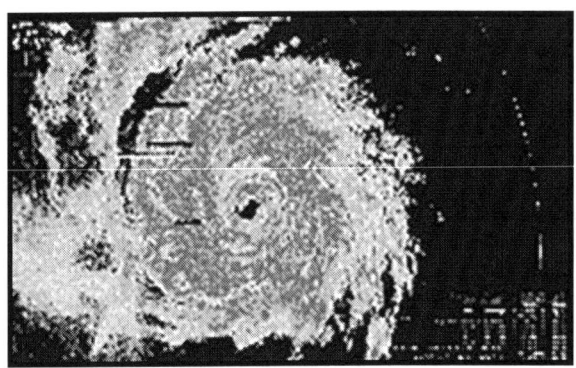

Radar image of Harvey as it approached.

BEFORE HARVEY: Frantic

August 22, 2017 Tuesday

Aransas County, TX

School maintenance personnel had been working in the buildings all day. They put away anything that could be a projectile, trimmed overhanging tree branches...standard storm preparation with no sense of urgency. Harvey seemed to be sluggish.

When Hurricane Harvey was just a tropical storm, I told my daughter I was coming to Austin. I got out my bag on Tuesday before the storm and left early Thursday morning. A tropical storm in the gulf with the water at 89 degrees will become a hurricane. I don't need a meteorologist to tell me that.

There is a common image that appears in many unlikely places, schoolrooms, biker bars, fences, all across Texas. "Texas Strong" is everywhere. As is the Texas flag ... the most recent one, at least. Who could have guessed

Not Gone With The Wind

on August 22, 2017 that within four days, "Rockport Strong" would become a common sight, on fences, debris piles, remains of homes and in print. And, as flagpoles were unearthed, the American flag and the Texas flag would be flying again.

There is a tropical depression somewhere around the Yucatan peninsula that looks like it may head into the Gulf of Mexico bringing rain. No big deal. But the EOC began meeting for updates from John Metz.

August 23, 2017 Wednesday, 10:15 am

Aransas County Emergency Operations Center

I live in Rockport; what's a little tropical storm? Besides, this ain't my first rodeo. I had been through Beulah 50 years ago.

Pre-Harvey Big Blue Crab at Little Bay

I am oblivious. I am not inside watching TV. Weather in Wisconsin is beautiful this time of year if you can ignore mosquitoes. Fishing is good.

Regularly scheduled meeting: John Metz, meteorologist with National Weather Service reports that Tropical Storm Harvey has moved into the Gulf of Mexico and is forecast to make landfall somewhere on the mid-Coast on Friday night or Saturday morning as a Category 1 hurricane.

Pre-Harvey Boarding Up

August 23, 2017 Wednesday, 4:15 pm

Aransas County

As a Winter Texan, I was oblivious. It was only another tropical storm that no one knew for sure where it was going.

Sports practices continued. Opening games were coming up. All my friends are ready! Sports are a really big deal to the Rockport-Fulton Pirates.

John Metz reported that Tropical Storm Harvey was moving very slowly with winds of 35 mph. There was concern about the amount of rain and the storm surge. Aransas County was the center of the cone of probability for the Category 1 Hurricane that might develop. All groups were preparing for a major storm, including AEP, ACND, ACISD, Rescue teams, Fire and Police departments, HEB and Walmart. Very few residents were paying attention. Hurricanes almost always landed east of Aransas County.

August 23, 2017 Wednesday, 10:15 pm

Aransas County Emergency Operations Center

We had been through hurricanes before all over the world, including typhoons in Okinawa. We would start worrying about it tomorrow.

As a Winter Texan, I was out of the country and paying no attention.

I have lived all over the world, weathered many storms, some worse than others like Andrew. Category 1 hurricanes are no big deal. My house is sturdy. I'm not going to fight the evacuation crowds. I'll be OK.

Homework...the first week of school...unfair! I have to do it or coach will make me pay in workout tomorrow.

John Metz reported that Harvey will develop into a Category 1 Hurricane and landfall is predicted between Rockport and Aransas Pass on Friday or Saturday. Preparations continue for a possible Category 1 hurricane. Residents in low-lying areas are advised to evacuate.

August 24, 2017 Thursday, 4:15 am

Aransas County Emergency Operations Center

Regularly scheduled meeting: Harvey has been upgraded to a tropical storm with winds of 45 mph. Hurricane warning and storm surge warning in effect for most of the area. Heavy rainfall predicted. Landfall predicted somewhere on the Texas Gulf Coast mid-Friday as a Category 1 hurricane with Rockport in the cone of probability.

August 24, 2017 Thursday, 10:15 am

Aransas County Emergency Operations Center

School had started, always a time of beginnings and change. Football and volleyball practice had started on 8/7/17. Band had been practicing since 7/31/17. Teachers had been in their classrooms since 8/10/17 getting ready. School started on Monday, 8/21/17 When announcements came of Harvey's path, school was dismissed Thursday at noon and evacuations started. No time ... no time ... no time to secure multiple buildings, to protect the contents ... no time to pack up band instruments, to protect athletic gear. Only time to for the schools' top priority ... the students. No disaster plan is designed to be implemented in 32 hours. Staff would have their own priorities once the students were safe... their own homes and families.

Not Gone With The Wind

The mandatory evacuation order came around 11:00 am and we began packing. You know, pack a lunch for the road to use up food, get a couple of days clothes...we wanted to be on the road by 6:00, heading for our hotel room in Luling. As news got worse, we hurried more. In the end, we ran out of time and did not put up the boards. We hoped for the best.

I was in assisted living for rehab after surgery when the mandatory evacuation began. I had no way to get to my house to board it up so I got people who said they would board it up for me. I gave them the locations of the panels and the hardware. But I couldn't get back to my house to get any money or papers before we were loaded on a bus for Austin. I hoped all would be OK.

I have lived in Rockport for 23 years, all in the same house, and this would be my third evacuation. No big

Pre-Harvey Rockport Art Center

Pre-Harvey Fulton Mansion

deal. I got my hair and my pedicure done and headed up the road to Austin. I had packed clothes for two days, gotten the house boarded up, and luckily had some paperwork with me. Business as usual.

Emergency responders from all over the United States began to head for Rockport, staging in areas that appeared to be safe from the worst of the hurricane, like Victoria and areas north of Houston. Best laid plans ... Harvey hit both areas. Electrical utility trucks, all sizes, with booms and some with a full load of power poles left towns and cities all over the United States. Travelers on interstates were amazed to see the convoys heading toward the gulf. Major evacuation routes couldn't be converted to one-way roads heading away from the hurricane; too many people and trucks were moving toward trouble.

Not Gone With The Wind

Friends who knew that my husband and I wintered in Rockport began calling. "Have you seen the Weather Channel?" When I turned it on, I was hooked. I watched constantly for days.

I evacuated! Disasters and I have shared space before ... announce a hurricane or floods ... I am gone. There isn't much to board up in a Park Model. I know when I leave that there may be nothing left when I get back. It has happened to me before; I will survive. But, maybe this time ...

I live in Rockport; why are there all those busses with people getting on? Perhaps I should check the weather news.

I live in Rockport. Suddenly, it was a Category 5 Hurricane but hurricanes here always go up the coast. This would go to Houston. They always did. No worries.

Late Thursday, Harvey was a Category 5 Hurricane. We started putting up shutters Thursday at 5:00 pm and we were still putting up shutters Friday at 3:30 am, in the rain ... with a flashlight. We were evacuating. No time to empty the refrigerators. We would later regret that a lot! We left town Friday at 8:00 am, through Victoria to Ft. Worth. We knew that traffic was backed up for 3 hours in San Antonio so we went up 77 to Waco. Not a lot better. We arrived in Ft. Worth at 5:00 pm.

My husband and I live in Canada and have been spending our winters in Rockport-Fulton for the past seven years. We have come to love the area and consider it our home away from home. As Winter Texans, of course, we did not experience Harvey first hand, but we have nonetheless been left with many vivid images. There was the radar image we watched back in Canada of Harvey gathering strength over the Gulf; a huge swirling mass of red, yellow and green bearing down inexorably on "our" Rockport. And we were powerless to do anything but watch.

My husband and I live in an RV Resort. We were debating about leaving when our son called and told us to "get out of Dodge!" and come to Marble Falls, TX. Then came the mandatory evacuation order. We pulled in the slides on our RV and then couldn't get the jacks to retract. The motor home stayed; the car left.

We are Winter Texans from Iowa, living in a trailer park. We evacuated on Thursday, taking our trailer with us, to Fredricksburg. We were fortunate to have the option of moving our trailer. Many people live in trailers that are permanently set and can only be moved by a hauling company. Our big pickup is our hauling company.

The owner of our trailer park is a doctor. She began telling staff to give their records to any patients who came in, since no one knew where they would end up, either the records or the patients.

I am a Rockport-Lamar transplant, sharing property with my son in Lamar. We originally were from Oklahoma and I will take a tornado any day compared to a hurricane. Especially a hurricane with tornadoes in it. Tornados come up quickly, do their damage and move on. Hurricanes just hang around for what seems like forever. So we evacuated to my son's place in Austin and watched Harvey on TV.

I did not evacuate, despite wanting to. I had four weiner dogs racing around like crazy. My father was on hospice. It was just too much to do, too little time.

25

Not Gone With The Wind

Pre- Harvey Rockport Band Shell

We are Rockport residents, formerly proud possessors of a big older house on Copano Bay. We evacuated, but not until the bridge tournament was over on Thursday. As a result, we got tangled up in the evacuation traffic getting to San Antonio. I thought that it would have been helpful if the four-way stops were eliminated on the evacuation route as well as the stoplight in the little town. Fewer evacuees would have thought of murder and mayhem when stuck for several hours in the lines.

We live in a trailer park and went to a dog-friendly motel in Fredricksburg under the mandatory evacuation. We knew that rain, flooding and storms follow the hurricane and we wanted to avoid them. Our friends evacuated to the same motel. We ate in the local restaurants and played duplicate bridge in Kerrville for 10 days. When the power went out, we knew that there was nothing we could do in Rockport.

Before Harvey: FRANTIC

We live in Rockport but had gone to Duluth, MN to visit great grandkids, a great thing to do for lots of Rockport residents ... a reverse migration from that of the Winter Texans. Heading home, we heard the radio report that said that Harvey was headed for Rockport. So we evacuated to friends in Abilene without ever getting back to Rockport. We were there when we learned that Rockport "had been hit in the nose" by Harvey.

I have lived in Rockport for many years. My house was built by the bridge builder of the Copano Bridge complete with concrete pillars. It should be fine. However, my 4 kids, 10 grandkids and 29 great grandkids voted that I would evacuate. I was just barely outnumbered. My son from San Antonio came to pack me up and take me away from danger in Rockport on August 24th. Since I would only be gone two days, I packed very little. He and I left and then he remembered the refrigerator and the freezers. Came back and he threw away all the contents. We left again. Credit cards are handy. I was back in my house by Christmas.

We closed the library on Thursday, crying because we knew that it might be gone when we got back. What do you take from a library when evacuating? The county backs up our records; my small car won't hold much; I chose two rare books as a place to start over our collection if I needed to.

Timing is everything. When we evacuated on August 24th we had only been back in our house for three weeks. A disastrous fire in February had led to rebuilding the house from the studs out. We had gotten hurricane resistant windows and doors, plank siding, new roof... new appliances, the works. We would now see if the claims were true.

Not Gone With The Wind

We evacuated to Fredricksburg late Thursday, five family members, 3 cats and a sugar glider. My 87 year old father wasn't leaving unless we took his truck so we were driving three vehicles. Crying became my default mode: crying because a cat was missing, crying because Rockport was being blown away, crying because my house might be gone. I was so depressed that I have almost no memories of the week we were gone.

And then there was the woman planning to stay put in her trailer. There were too many family members and pets to put in her small car. But the message came from her truck driver husband to get out of town as fast as she could. So, she loaded her mother and two grown daughters in the back seat of her small car. The 140 pound bull mastiff stretched across their laps and one daughter held the hamster. A grown son was in the front seat with the English Bull Dog. The parakeet rode on her shoulder. She announced to all, humans and pets, that once they got the big dog's tail in and the door closed, that they would not be stopping until they had a motel room. The pit stop implications were clear. They found a motel room several hours up the road and stayed in one room for two weeks. A tribute to human ingenuity and to the motel owners' willingness to stretch every rule in the book.

My family evacuated to Austin. My kids called it an e-vacation. They didn't enroll in another district but did work on-line until January.

I am evacuating. My son has room for me. My neighbor asks if she could come also. I call my son. "Sure, bring her along." My neighbor comes back and asks if she can bring her three dogs. I call my son. The silence is a bit longer. "Oh sure, bring them too. It will just be for two or three days." Two days later, he returned to my house in Rockport to get the rest of my medicine, empty the freezer, and tar the roof. Minimal damage but two days turned into two weeks. Family is priceless.

I live in Rockport in a trailer home. I was ready to leave. I don't ride out hurricanes. Getting ready to load my dog and cat when my handicapped neighbor asked for a ride out of the storm. Really no decision ... I loaded up my neighbor and left the dog and cat. They survived but the cat didn't speak to me for a month.

I live in Rockport: word came about the evacuation. We had thought we might go but were in no hurry. Suddenly, it was a mandatory evacuation and we had 45 minutes to get out. We threw stuff into the motor home with no plan and left town.

As a Winter Texan, I was called by my son to see if I was watching the Weather Channel. I spent the next days glued to the television, with the same fascination as those who watch train wrecks. I called my Rockport landlord and we agreed to wait to cash my deposit until we saw if there would be a place to return to. I rent a little beach cottage, just off Little Bay. Built in 1958, sitting on concrete blocks, I was not optimistic.

When we first heard about the storm in the Wednesday afternoon EOC meeting, it was still a tropical storm, possible winds up to 80 mph, coming in sometime Saturday morning somewhere on the Gulf Coast between Corpus Christi and Port Lavaca. School maintenance personnel had begun Tuesday securing anything that might get blown about, trimming trees with overhanging limbs. Between Wednesday at 4:00 pm and Thursday at 10:15 am, Harvey became a Category 3 or 4 hurricane heading straight for Rockport on Friday evening. I called from the meeting to begin cancelling school at noon.

School busses were then moved to Sinton to higher ground. All students and staff were gone from the schools by 3:30 on Thursday so I went home to start boarding up. The Board Meeting for the budget was at 7:00 that night. Couldn't cancel that. I showed up in my work clothes, the budget was passed, and we left at 7:30 for family in New Braunfels.

6

Regularly scheduled meeting: John Metz said he had bad news and worse news. The bad news: He reported that Harvey would at least be a Category 4. The worse news: Harvey would be making landfall in Rockport within 32 hours. Harvey had grown from a Category 1 hurricane to a Category 4 in about 6 hours. In fact, predictions for a Category 5 were made.

The EOC has a large square set of tables that will seat several on a side. The people who are in charge of major departments or institutions all have assigned seats around the table. No skipping a meeting without the absence being blazingly obvious. Sort of "a death in the family better be yours" situation. Then there is another larger square set of tables outside the first set. Each administrator has an assistant sitting right behind him, often taking notes for the boss. There will also be other administrators in this set of tables, again each with an assigned seat. And finally, there is an outer ring of people with specific duties, often involving communication. For example, Diane Probst, Rockport-Fulton Chamber of Commerce, has the ability to instantly notify all members of the status of the storm. Word can be spread rapidly through the Chamber. Meetings are mandatory when a disaster has been declared. Everyone

Home and shop damage

gets the same information at the same time. Very efficient. Very interesting to watch when John Metz announces that a Category 4 or 5 hurricane will be in Rockport in 32 hours. Administrators froze, looked at their assistants, and people in the outer ring raced out, phones in hand.

The Superintendent of Schools was stunned and turned to his assistants. Cancel school immediately and get everyone home so they can evacuate.

The Nursing Home coordinators bolted with the first bad news ... a Category 4 hurricane meant that all residents had to be evacuated immediately along with the staff to care for the residents.

Rockport moved the operations center for the city to Bastrop, TX , southeast of Austin, to secure continuity of government. Mayor Wax went to Bastrop; Mayor Pro Tem Rios stayed in Rockport. Nursing homes began evacuating busloads of patients to sister facilities where shelters had been set up for their patients. All county, city, school and business maintenance personnel moved into high gear to secure the facilities. Homeowners began putting up plywood. Key Allegro's standard procedure is to issue a mandatory evacuation order because of the area's vulnerability to storm surge and hurricane winds. When the mandatory evacuation order was issued for all of the Aransas County area, many people left to safety. People stayed, as they always do, and prepared for a storm. Business owners began to secure their records and inventory. Some made certain to acquire generators stored, in some cases, out of the predicted landfall zone. So much to do; so little time.

Hotel damage along Broadway beside Little Bay

DURING HARVEY: Survival

August 25, 2017 Friday afternoon

Aransas County, TX

It was too late. We couldn't evacuate. My 86 year old father refused to leave. My 13 June Project rescued dogs were in various stages of rehabilitation and would have had to be moved individually. Volunteers couldn't get in to get them out in time in their special cages. I had to stay.

I live in Rockport and work at Rockport Donuts. Matthew, the owner, Alex and I did not evacuate. We spent our time preparing our buildings. There was supposed to be flooding so we piled

Home damage Rockport

Not Gone With The Wind

three feet of sand in the doors of the shop and our other building and put up boards on the windows. Then we prepared to wait it out.

We were in Canada. We could only watch as the hurricane built, knowing that we probably would not have our park model trailer to come home to in October.

We are in Nebraska and our beloved 5th wheel is in Rockport. We are watching the Weather Channel compulsively ... for three days. What could go wrong did go wrong. We were sure that nothing could survive. But we had hope ...

I live in Rockport. A mandatory evacuation and my husband refuses to leave. I have too many responsibilities, too many people and pets depending on me. I can't make up my mind to leave. I'd rather take my chances on a hurricane than the crazies on the road trying to evacuate. There isn't enough time ...

I live in Rockport. I wanted to evacuate but my father was in hospice with COPD and I couldn't get him moved in time. Not enough lead time, no EMS, no emergency evacuation. He was dependent on oxygen and I knew that without power, he would die. The storm was closing in when I loaded him up and took him to Live Oak shelter. From there, he was transferred several times and the stress was too much for him. He died the week after Harvey.

I am beginning to have second thoughts about staying but it is too late to leave. The outer bands are bringing wind and rain. About 6:30 pm the phone rings; my friend in Corpus wants me to get out of Rockport and come to her spare room. I threw a few things in the car and left. The hurricane force wind and rain on the road were frightening; I gripped the steering wheel so hard that my hands were bleeding by the time I arrived in Corpus, a 35 mile drive.

Lighthouse Inn After Harvey

I had lived in New Mexico and West Texas before coming to Rockport. I work for the city of Fulton in maintenance. My teammate and I had been driving around Fulton securing all the city buildings while waiting for Harvey to hit. By about 7:30, the wind was up to 75 mph and the rain was getting bad so we decided to check in to the Fairfield Hotel.

Mayor Wax announces that everyone should leave. If you were going to stay, put your name and social security number on your arm in permanent ink so you could be identified. Made the national news.

9

Emergency responders are in place; utility trucks staged outside the zone; National Guard in place; large contingents of police heading to staging areas from all over; City Hall functions moved to Bastrop Tx; essential personnel hunkered down in the Service Center. Nursing home residents evacuated, along with their records and their nurses who followed their patients. School busses evacuated to Sinton. No way to evacuate police vehicles; they were essential but vulnerable. Rockport was in survival mode. But no one really knew that Harvey was going to be different....very different.

A hurricane is supposed to make landfall at its maximum strength, Category 4 for example, and then begin to lose strength almost immediately as it moves across the land. The warm water of the Gulf of Mexico, in Harvey's case, fueled the storm. Deprived of fuel, Harvey should have moved and diminished. It didn't. The eye of a hurricane often moves over a single spot in 30 minutes

Storage units and contents after Harvey

to an hour. It didn't. Two high pressure systems bracketed Harvey and held it in place ... over Rockport, near enough to warm water to refuel ... for 13 hours. Devastation was incredible.

Winds: 142 mph measured at the airport just before the storm took down the equipment. We may not know for sure if Harvey was a Category 4 or 5. Meteorologists estimated winds over 220 mph in the eye wall. Duration: forever in hurricane terms. 13 hours of hurricane force winds of over 75 mph in Rockport. Eye took 2.5 hours to pass over a single point. Damage: catastrophic wind damage in Rockport, Fulton, and Aransas County; water damage in specific areas on Copano Bay. The good news about water damage is that, given time, water will go away on its own. The bad news about wind damage: the resulting debris will have to be hauled off. No one could have predicted the amount of debris that Harvey would generate in Aransas County.

Oyster House Restaurant (formerly Alice Faye's)

August 25-26, 2017 Friday night-Saturday morning

Aransas County, TX

I live in Rockport. 4:00 am and it was now a Cat 4 Hurricane zeroing in on Rockport. We loaded the camper and the truck, packed the dog, headed to Del Rio and then Riudoso, New Mexico. We left the rest of the animals to fend for themselves and stayed for a month.

The hurricane was coming and my friends had decided to stay. Their house was secured and they waited. Then they heard a knock on the door. My friend looked out the window but couldn't see anyone outside. He opened the door and there were three big raccoons, banging on the door. Later, a possum knocked. They knew ... they knew.

Stripes station at entrance to Key Allegro

As a Winter Texan, I had resigned myself to finding another place to winter this year. I began my search when I saw the path of the hurricane. But I found that I was suddenly picky. Phoenix-Tucson: too hot. No ocean. Brownsville: too hot. Florida: too expensive. Mississippi: meh. I could stay home; Kansas in the winter is ... is ... cold. What I wanted was ocean, warmth, trees, birds, fish and my friends. I wanted Rockport.

I am still watching the news, watching mammoth red and orange Harvey coming closer and closer to Rockport.

RV Park after Harvey

We are settled in our hotel room but we now know how serious this storm is. We may not have anything to return to, certainly not in the two or three days we planned for. Neither my husband nor I could stand the thought of spending two to four weeks in a hotel, doing nothing but watching the news. Where could we go? Relatives on either coast; military friends in South Dakota. Friends won out, just a straight shot north. We knew we needed the emotional support our friends could give us if our house was gone. We left the next day.

I really wanted to leave. I am not the type to just tough it out. However, I had my first round of chemotherapy on August 24th and I was instructed to be prone for 48 hours. So I stayed. An elderly relative came to help me but the stress was too much for her. She died shortly after Harvey.

I own an electrical business in New Braunfels, northeast of San Antonio, but I am often in Rockport in our second home. It is a little place but has all my wife and I need. My boat, my RV, my other essentials are

East facing side of home in Holiday Beach

usually in Rockport. When news came about the tropical storm, I wasn't worried. Button everything up and all would be well. I checked with the New Orleans relatives, veterans of Katrina, who checked the weather news. "Get your stuff and get out right now!" was the verdict. With the help of friends, we got everything out and back to New Braunfels. Sitting on the deck on Saturday, enjoying a glass of wine, I heard from New Orleans. I told them all was well and I was just sitting waiting. Waiting for what? The Category 1 Hurricane Harvey that was coming into New Braunfels in another hour.

A housekeeper at Econolodge worked to get everyone evacuated from the facility on Friday. After the last customer left, she locked up and realized that she didn't have enough gas to get out of town to safety. So she and her family huddled in a closet in her home and braced the walls of the closet. In the morning, all that was left standing of her house was the closet.

As a Winter Texan, I continued my vigil, as though witnessing would somehow mitigate the damage. I saw pieces of structures that I recognized blown about; I saw weather people blown about; I worried about who and what I did not see.

Aransas County Courthouse after Harvey

We stayed, and because we had worked with firefighters, we had a scanner. We listened to updates and calls as long as there was power for the responders. After the towers went down, there was darkness and silence. Except for the wind …

The storm developed so fast that, as volunteer firemen,

we had no time to evacuate the trucks. So we got them all in the building. When the wind hit, the big doors began to bulge in. It was just a matter of time before they would blow in. So, we pulled the fire trucks up tight to the doors. It worked. The doors held.

I live in Rockport; I did not evacuate. As experiences go, I have decided to never repeat it. It was good that we were there to fix the window that blew in; it was bad when the power went out and we were left in the dark ... pitch dark. No light, no phone, no news. I remembered my LED votive candles and we put one in every room so we wouldn't hurt ourselves. I still am more comfortable with one or two burning all night. I don't like the dark.

We have five dogs and a cat. We couldn't leave. I sat in my recliner with my little dog. My husband sat in his with his big dog with the health issues. Since there was no thunder, the animals slept through the whole thing. We should have been so lucky.

I live in Rockport; I did not evacuate, despite family turmoil. My father's word was "you always stay to take care of the property. If you don't, there will be nothing left." My daughter had left Friday morning to fly overseas to see her husband in the military, leaving the two granddaughters with us. The son-in-law, monitoring the situation through military communication channels, demanded that we evacuate to Houston with the two granddaughters. We stayed, the granddaughters went to Houston, and relations are still strained over our decision to stay. In the end, we were both safe.

I just slept through the whole thing. Anonymous
    His house was relatively intact. Hearing loss has its advantages.

Home damage in Lamar

Matthew, Alex and I finished prepping our buildings, checked into the Holiday Inn Express and hoped for the best. To Matthew's surprise, I went to sleep during the front half of the hurricane. I said my prayers and said if it's going to take me, make it while I am asleep. When the eye came through, we went out and walked around and looked at the damage. Nothing could be done so we went back to the hotel. Then the backside hit and building began to shake and sway in the wind.

I had watched the storm build from our hotel room. We were the only residents in the hotel. Palms bending in the wind; rain lashing across the parking lot but not much sound in our room. Then the windows began to vibrate; the walls shivered. Terrifying. I hated to wake up Alex and Billy but when the eye came through, I thought we should go outside and check on things. The air was still and the sound of the frogs and crickets was almost deafening. I'll

Tree damage at Goose Island State Park, Lamar

never forget that sound. Then came the back of the storm. I only thought I was scared before that.

Home damage Holiday Beach

The eye was coming and my friend with EMS got word out somehow that they were taking vehicles out during the eye to try to help people. I went out to check on people. The water was knee-deep the closer I got to Little Bay. There was so much brush and debris that I couldn't get down my street. The National Guard came out as soon as the storm was over and began moving the debris into piles so emergency vehicles could get down the street. I had no power and no communications.

We live in Rockport and evacuated to San Antonio. I had never really liked Facebook but I do now. The only news we could get out of Rockport was through Facebook. Patty Rios also evacuated but maintained an information line through her husband, the mayor pro tem. She constantly was passing information on all night and throughout our stay. Facebook was a lifeline to me.

We are Rockport residents and we stayed. We live in the middle of five acres of oak trees, a bit isolated. We did all we could to prepare, covered the windows, and sat back to wait. I felt the house begin to shake a bit, then a lot. I told my husband that I loved him. He replied that he loved me too. And that if we survived the night, we would still love each other in the morning.

We live in Refugio but are members of the Woman's Club. We did not evacuate. We did not put up boards or shutters but we did have a newer metal roof with the metal tied down every twelve inches. If that roof was going to go, it would take the whole house with it. We got up in the middle of the storm; it was pitch black and we could hear the tornados around us. The roof survived. So did we.

Horrified, we watched the news. How could any trailer withstand the winds that were devastating hotels? Nothing to be done but hope.

When the eye of Harvey passed over the trailer park, one of the residents reported that you could hear the water being sucked up through the trailer's plumbing, including the septic system. Who knew?

Rockport-Fulton High School Gym

Not Gone With The Wind

Power was out in Corpus Christi. I didn't see the storm pictures. That may not have been a bad thing.

I was incensed; as a Winter Texan in Canada, I wanted to know what was happening in Rockport. The day after Harvey left Rockport, CBS, NBC and their counterparts left also. The news was all in Houston. No further information about Rockport was available to me on national media.

Condos damaged near Copano Village

I don't know how to tell when the hurricane is over. The eye should be half way. What if you aren't in the eye exactly but sort of ... not ever completely silent ... not ever completely windless ... not ever a clear switch in wind directions? What if the hurricane doesn't know where it is going and so just sits there destroying your life and your home and your business? What if it feels like Hurricane Harvey will never end, even after four months have passed?

When I wondered about where the birds went, I was told that birds sometimes got into the eye of the hurricane and stayed there, traveling wherever the hurricane went. A bit like a giant bird vacuum cleaner. When the eye collapses, the survivors may head back home ... or not.

We lost power about 7:00 pm on Friday. We lost cell phone service at 11:20. We were alone in the dark with

13 rescued dogs. Our house was flooding with water from the rain, not the ocean as expected; our roof was disintegrating; trees were crashing down outside. We had no way of communicating with the people trying to see if we were still alive. We weren't entirely sure that we would be, come morning.

My friend's apartment is on the 10th floor of a high rise apartment building ... on top of what passes for a cliff in Corpus Christi. The sound of the storm winds felt like an attack on the building. I lived in her spare room for two weeks. My decision to evacuate was the right one. My house in Rockport was destroyed.

We had evacuated essential city services to Bastrop when it became clear that Harvey was going to be a major event. On Saturday, August 26, I spent thirteen hours on my cell phone in Bastrop talking to people from as far away as New Zealand. I released my cell phone number so I could handle the calls. People wanting to talk to the mayor or the police chief or the emergency operations coordinator talked to the Mayor. It seemed more important that the Mayor Pro Tem concentrate on the immediate needs, police chief concentrate on his job and that the Emergency Management Coordinator deal with emergency operations. I won answering the phone.

Many of the weather people in town booked rooms in the Fairfield Inn, a new hotel in Rockport,

Home along waterfront in Copano Village

built to withstand Category 5 hurricanes. Those of us glued to news feeds during Harvey watched weather folk evacuating the hotel. It was not comforting to see adrenaline junkies frightened.

We stayed with the 13 rescued dogs in my house rather than the clinic. I had worried about the wind, rightfully so, but not for the reason that I thought. My storage barns began to disintegrate and my clinic was badly damaged by projectiles from my own barns. When the chimney in my house was ripped off, water began to pour in the house like a fire hose. We couldn't bail fast enough to get ahead of it. I could hear the metal peeling off the roof on my house. During the eye, I went out my front door to find lumber to raise the dogs' cages in case of more flooding and could see nothing but green metal from the roof in the yard along with the other debris

Homes damaged in Copano Village

I watched the wind from our third floor window at the Fairfield, bending the palm trees and I knew that they would break soon. The walls began to vibrate and then to shake. I went to sit in a chair and felt it move like the climb on a roller coaster; I went back to the window. The manager came by and asked people to meet in the dining area. As I went down the stairwell, I saw sheetrock fragments and looked up. The back of the building was separating from the rest of the building. It looked like the wall was breathing, in and out, in and out. We knew that we would need to get people out during the eye.

There is a concrete block school building down the street and so we thought to try to find a path that people could take from the hotel. My teammate opened the hotel door and I heard a familiar sound from my West Texas days. I grabbed him away from the door and we watched a little tornado going down the road. Finally the eye came and the silence was soothing but not the sights. So many power lines; so much debris; so many trees blocking the road. Finally got a path and began taking people from the hotel to the shelter, getting the last of those who wanted to go in just before the back of the hurricane hit. Many of the storm chasers stayed in the hotel. I'd be lying if I said that I wasn't scared.

Harvey made landfall in Aransas County on Friday, August 25, 2017 around 7:30 pm. Conditions had begun deterioriating in the afternoon. Most people who were leaving, were gone. Most people who were staying (40% of the population) were hunkered down. Essential personnel for Rockport were in the Service Center; EOC personnel were in the Public Service Center; firemen were in the firehouses; police were on the streets initially but as the wind rose over 80 mph, they returned to safer places. Unfortunately, their vehicles were outside. As the storm built and the wind rose, people in the Public Service Center began hearing sirens. Impossible! All officers were in the building. Flashing lights too ... The wind had broken out the windows in the emergency vehicles and the rain had

Not Gone With The Wind

shorted out all the electronics, setting off the sirens and all the lights. Spooky ... but just part of a night of terror.

Attempts were made to get out during the eye to try to locate the emergencies called in to 911. Dispatchers had the heartbreaking task of telling people that they had no way to get help to them until the wind died down. Many of the people who stayed instead of evacuating were without families or places to go or operating vehicles to get them there. With typical Texan independence, they figured that they could just ride it out. No one really expected a storm like Harvey became. Remarkably, there was no death directly attributed to the hurricane.

The Emergency Operations Center, located in the Public Service Center, was a secure place to wait out the hurricane. The communications center was in place. The EOC and the National Weather Service sent out warnings on social media up until the power went out about 7:30 pm. There was a redundancy of eight different ways to get the word out ... cell phones, satellite phones, VHF, Ham radio. Each had weaknesses; for example, satellite phones need clear skies to send a message. But surely one of these would work.

When the eye passed and the wind direction immediately switched, every one of these was gone at once. Completely. Nothing.

While Harvey took out communications

Home hidden by downed trees at Goose Island

in the EOC, people with cell phones could sometimes get a signal. There was a satellite phone with the Mayor Pro Tem, Pat Rios but not much clear sky. News often couldn't get relayed until someone physically left Rockport and found cell phone service. Not possible until Harvey moved on. A Social Media relay became the primary way to let friends and relatives know that everything was OK and to get news to the outside world for several days.

At daybreak, when the winds began to die down, Rick McLester, Emergency Management Coordinator and his crew headed out to the highest spot in the county, the airport, to see if they could get a signal. Amazingly, they got a faint cell signal and called the District Disaster Coordinator, Brandi Fisher, in Corpus Christi.

"I need the Package."

"It's on the way."

Tree damage in Copano Village

RV Park near Goose Island

Senior Center in downtown Fulton

THE AFTERMATH: DISASTER

August 26-August 28, 2017 Saturday-Monday

Without power, it seemed that an old-fashioned bulletin board in places where people gathered would be a good idea. Post the Mayor's letters there. Maybe next time.

We evacuated to New Mexico and our only news was from YouTube, Facebook and rumors.

I kept seeing people parked on the Hwy 35 overpass. One driver would stop and then there would be five or six trucks all lined up. A mystery soon explained. Someone had gotten a cell phone signal and now they were all getting news, some from friends and some from social media. Without power, there was no news.

The Rockport Post Office was destroyed. For a small town, there are an enormous number of PO Boxes to serve Winter Texans and others ... in the post office. Home mailboxes have been destroyed by the storm and then buried under debris. Street signs are gone.

House numbers are gone. Mail trucks are damaged or destroyed. Mail carriers evacuated and then couldn't return because of the debris. Other vendors couldn't deliver packages. Initially, mail was not an alternative to damaged digital communication networks.

One good thing about the curfew: any vehicle coming down the street at night with lights on better have emergency lights also. Otherwise, they would be pulled over for violating the curfew. We picked up a number of drug dealers for violating curfew.

I was called back to Corpus Christi where I worked for an electric company and thought I would be able to stay in our home. No power ... ironic when you work for an electric company. No air-conditioning ... not possible to stay in our home so I moved to my office. Except for the

Marriott Hotel, built to withstand a Cat 5, East wall collapsed before Harvey's Eye Wall passed

motion sensor that went off regularly all night long, it was better than the heat. I missed my family.

After I got information to the District Disaster Coordinator, trained disaster management people began to pour in to Rockport. Here came the cavalry!

Harvey changed the school district's business-as-usual relationship with our insurers. One of the early phone calls that I got in New Braunfels was from North Star Recovery, the district's disaster recovery organization, on Saturday saying that they were on their way. Our Maintenance Director got to Rockport on Saturday and began to take pictures of the damage to the school buildings. After he got to power again, he sent videos with the message "it's worse than it looks on TV." North Star was there assessing the damage; it would take 4 or 5 days before they could complete the assessment. Then more time to estimate repair time. I had no answers for the students and parents who called about when school would start up again. I hate saying "I don't know."

    The worst is over but there is widespread damage and unbelievable debris. The Mayor requests that people who evacuated not come back as there are no services. There is a curfew from 7 pm to 7 am, enforced by National Guard, Police and Sheriff. Six thousand electric workers in the city, all with trucks. With no communication, rumor circulates wildly. Contrary to rumor, there is no widespread looting and no multiple deaths. Texas Task Force 1 reports that 30-40% of houses and businesses in Rockport are completely destroyed; another 30% cannot be rebuilt. The Service

Center out on Hwy 35 was built in 2014 to withstand wind and water events. It did its job; staff lived in the resource center for wo weeks. The support center normally takes 250-300 calls a day with two operators; during Harvey and the aftermath, it handled 4200-4600 calls a day. Cities from all over Texas mobilized to send trained personnel to help handle the emergencies. The city staff was dealing with the same issues as other Rockport residents; 28 out of 132 were now homeless.

After Rick McLester, the local Emergency Operations Coordinator, got information to Brandi Fisher, the District Disaster Coordinator, she began to expand the request for help. Aransas County is part of the Corpus Christi region for Emergency Management . After the call for "the package", Brandi sent out the call for help to all the resources in the region and police/fire/ambulance crews began to mobilize. Next step up was the state resources. Word went out statewide; Aransas County had been hammered.

Without power, TV news was not an option for most people. News withdrawal began to set in. People who had not

Side view of the Rockport Art Center

seen the value in smartphones began to wish for one. Mayor Wax's letters were available on the internet but only to those outside of the city. A curfew was in place but the people who stayed had no idea. They didn't want to be out after dark anyway.

The Rockport Post Office was destroyed and would have to be gutted and rebuilt.

Twenty-four hours after the communications went out, the computer tech located the only dial tone, buried in the circuits of the PSC. It was on an old land line, copper wire, buried, and forgotten. It was barely functional but until then, there had been no way to get any word out from the EOC that anyone had survived.

The early pictures on the media showed the high school gym destroyed. Pretty hard to board up a gymnasium. Later pictures weren't as graphic but the announcement from the superintendent that schools would be closed indefinitely because there was no timeline for a full recovery stunned everyone. The damage was so extensive and affected every building in ACISD. The school year might be over before it ever got going.

The water towers had been full before the hurricane hit. By daybreak, the towers were empty. Where had the water gone? A massive leak was suspected and searched for ... no big leak. But what was found was 13,000 small leaks where water was still flowing into destroyed structures. Utility workers worked frantically to close water meter valves so the towers could refill. A corresponding problem: when water comes in and people begin using it, sewers soon become a necessity ... very soon. Pumping stations don't work without power. A sewer system has a large number of pumping stations of various sizes. Generators are not routinely installed throughout a system; it is too expensive and would rarely be needed. Bring on the generators! Public Works employees were exhausted.

Blue tarps on Bay House Condos

Boat in damaged Boat Barn

EARLY RESPONDERS

I am a Rockport resident; I did not evacuate. My father's warnings to the contrary, I did not see any looting. There were police, fire, National Guard, sheriff...all kinds of security...there immediately when the wind and rain died down. We had to show our driver's license to be allowed into our area. First responders came by every day to see if we needed anything. I felt safe.

Over the years, our son played with Rescue Heroes and, as kids do, left them in the yard. I had always picked them up and put them in the latticework around the porch. After the hurricane, we saw that the Rescue Heroes were still there, in the lattice, guarding the house.

Grocery stores may not be what I first think of as First Responders but HEB certainly responded very quickly. The disaster team from headquarters in San Antonio

HEB grocery store in Rockport - one the first businesses to reopen.

arrived on Sunday with generators and began inspecting and stabilizing the store's structure; employees from other stores arrived on Monday to clean out and restock the store. Local employees started on Tuesday. The mobile kitchens began handing out food on Monday. There was a drive thru loop with the first stop to pick up meals, next stop bread and ice and water. There was a line also as soon as gas was available, not only for cars but also for generators. People had been going to Portland for gas before HEB was open.

It was Sunday, first full day after Harvey, and the curfew was in effect, 7 am to 7 pm. About 6:30, I heard vehicles trying to get in our driveway. Concealed carry is the law in Texas and I was always armed so I was not afraid, just curious. I climbed through the debris and walked toward the road. A group approached the driveway and asked if I was the veterinarian. Who wanted to know, I wondered. Then they introduced themselves. They were First Responders from Bastrop, 3 hours away, sent by my friends to see if I was alive.

Walgreen's was severely damaged; WalMart had extensive damage; HEB had damage. We had no pharmacies operating in Rockport. I told HEB about the problem and they brought in generators and operated a mobile pharmacy along with the rest of their disaster team. Truly a lifesaver.

While my family evacuated, I stayed in Rockport to man the jail. While all the prisoners had been transferred to College Station, the Police Station and the jail served as home base for First Responders. Mercy Chefs fed us. My family worried since we had no power and no transmission ability after Harvey hit. I wished that I could reassure them but I wasn't sure that I really would be all right.

The Aftermath: DISASTER

In a disaster, there are several kinds of early responders. There are First Responders. These are people who are hired and trained to do certain tasks to aid people in need. These include police, fire, National Guard and ambulance crews as well as all the support staff like dispatchers. They will have direct contact with people in need and have chosen to be in a position of danger. Their training will have been fairly specific but when the disaster strikes, they react to meet the needs they encounter. For example, volunteer firemen use the winch on their trucks to move power poles and live wires blocking the road so that ambulance crews can get through.

Businesses have disaster response teams as well. Their jobs may be dangerous but may not involve a great deal of contact with the public. American Electric Power, Texas is a subsidiary of AEP, the electrical utility. Each of the sister companies has a mutual assistance agreement and has their own disaster teams, ready to provide assistance as soon as needed. The local coordinator is in charge of housing, feeding and fueling the incoming trucks and workers. This was almost impossible in Rockport and most workers stayed in Corpus Christi. AEP prepares for disasters months in advance. For example, throughout the AEP system, the contracts for staging areas are negotiated far ahead and are in place whether the areas are needed or not. Teams from sister companies headed into the area when it first became obvious that a disaster was in the making and were staged outside the area affected by Harvey.

HEB has disaster teams in place for any store that needs help. Each store in the network has employees that volunteer to be on the local disaster team, not primarily for their own store, but to travel to stores in disaster areas.

Not Gone With The Wind

The equipment and supplies that they need are kept ready all the time at the headquarters in San Antonio and the trucks head out to be ready when it is possible to get into the affected area. The first team enters the store to secure the area and check the safety of the building; these are permanent crews that mobilize only for disasters. In the case of Harvey, they were in the store on Sunday. Work began on temporary repairs to assure the safety of the building and work crews; additional crews to clean out the store were in on Monday. Local employees were called back in on Tuesday to begin preparing the store to open and to offer services, including food, ice, water in the parking lot by Tuesday. The store opened on Thursday, August 31, 2017.

Then there are early responders who, despite lack of specific disaster training, see a need and fill it. They may be a neighbor who sees that trees are blocking the exit from another home and helps to move the limb. They may be volunteers who saw the storm on television and headed toward the disaster area with a truck load of tools. They may be maintenance personnel who ferry people to safety from an unsafe building. Some are neighbors who can only offer a hug because their house is gone also; others come in vehicles with flashing red lights with city names that you can't even locate. Businesses like ACE Hardware opened almost immediately, turned on

Storm surge damage in Copano Village

generators and were providing supplies almost before the rain stopped. First Responders or early responder, all initial responses are local, geared to protecting and assisting individuals; property comes in a distant second.

When the call went to Brandi Fisher for "the package", First Responders had been watching the situation and just needed information about where to go first. There were search and rescue teams with dogs, including a team from Mexico. There were law enforcement personnel from all over the state. There were fire departments with vehicles loaded with tools like chainsaws, rakes, winches to help clear debris so that people who needed help could get it. There were dispatchers. There were emergency management coordinators who could assist in this animal called Harvey. Finally, First Responders in Aransas County who had been awake for 72 hours could take a break.

Neighbors helping neighbors; the brotherhood formed by people doing similar jobs in different places; the urge to race to danger to help; the foresight to have a system that can stretch to fit even a massive storm like Harvey. Without all of these factors, the disaster that was Harvey in Aransas County would have been a catastrophe from which the area could not recover.

August 28 - September 9, 2017,

Aransas County

I was horrified by the pictures of the devastation taken from the air that were shown on TV soon after the hurricane. It looked at first as though little was left of the town. It was a good thing that I watched it early on ... by Sunday afternoon, there was no more news coverage of Rockport or Aransas County.

Not Gone With The Wind

I evacuated, with my handicapped neighbor. My trailer survived with damage. Twenty-seven trailers in my park were lost immediately. We even had one RV up a tree.

I rode out the storm, not by choice. I began sorting debris ... wood ... plastic ... wood ... plastic. It was mindless but gave me a sense of having some control over the situation.

As a Winter Texan, I pored over YouTube, looking for "my" house that we have rented several times in Fulton. Success! ... or not. Half of the roof had blown off and the carport was gone. With so many people homeless and so many contractors in town, would we be able to find anywhere to stay?

We were amazed that our shop had so little damage ... just a little wet spot near the windows. I began shoveling away the sand from the doors. One of my church members came by and said "All I could see was asses and

Downed trees blocking the road near Goose Island

elbows." We opened for business immediately. All we had was coffee and kolaches that we handed out from the drive-through window. We had two small generators at first and then a customer brought by a generator large enough to power the whole shop. People began to crowd in for hot food. Then is when part of the ceiling collapsed.

Hit or Miss examples near Goose Island

Our building was new and built to code so I was sure it would be all right and it was. We had the small generators so we began using the supplies on hand to fix food. We were the first restaurant to reopen on Sunday. We had to; our business has to keep operating or it will not be able to pay its bills. But we had to go to Robstown originally to get fuel for the generators; our food supplies had to come from Corpus. My wife and I were running the business during the day and getting supplies at night. We were exhausted. When the federal official came and accused us of price gouging since we had raised our price for a donut from $.75 to $1.00 to cover fuel costs, I was ready to shut down. I was talked out of it and I was assured later that the official had no right to even ask the question. It was a city issue. And a power issue that didn't involve electricity.

We stayed and the storm nearly did us in. My husband lost 20 lbs in the first week, mostly from depression. We had no communication. The isolation was intense. We finally got out of the house to survey the damage despite the flattened front porch blocking the front door and the big trees down by the back door. We saw a friend coming to check on us, followed by two EMS vehicles that they asked to come along. With no communication, she was afraid we were dead.

I feel like I am on information overload. I am watching videos, looking for places I recognize. I looked for the Woman's Club but the film always stopped just before it got to that intersection. On the Wharf ... all the huts are gone. The Wildcat is gone. Boats are jumbled ... no Woman's Club pictures. What happened?

When we returned, we found that the rebuilt house had minimal damage. If not for the fire the February before and the rebuilding after, we think the house would have

Debris ... DeBRIS ... DEBRIS !!!

been destroyed as were other houses in our neighborhood. Sometimes blessings are hard to recognize until later.

Every place has something in Holiday Beach

We came back on Monday, August 28, and started in to work on the clean-up. One of the residents who did not evacuate got completely blown out of his trailer when the front side peeled away. "I just rolled around like a Dixie Cup in the wind." Another resident was the self-appointed guard of a section of the park. He sat in the Pool Hall with a gun for two weeks until his kids came and got him.

Our house survived with minimal damage but the yard was a war zone. Trees blocked the driveway. There was no power in Refugio. A neighbor got in with water and a generator. We are on Rural Electric and we had power restored in three days. The town was still without power for six weeks.

We started back from Austin and I didn't see real signs of Harvey until we reached Goliad. Then we began to see all the downed power lines. We knew that it would take a long time to restore power. Then we saw our houses

Not Gone With The Wind

... or we saw trees down everywhere and somewhere in there were our houses. When we finally walked in through the debris, we saw that the houses had survived. But oh, the trees ... we lost at least 50 big live oaks completely, blown out of the ground. Then there were all the smaller trees that were shattered. What to do?

My friends and I made it through Harvey in Corpus but now we had another problem. We are in a high rise apartment building; there is no power. No power means no elevators. No elevators means walking up and down 10 flights of stairs. There was nothing that we needed badly enough to do that. We didn't leave the apartment for 3 days. It felt like a very nice, attractive, prison.

More damage in Holiday Beach

My nephew in Tivoli went to Rockport to check on my house on Key Allegro. He sent a picture ... no roof, no front, no side, furniture tangled outside. I didn't need an adjuster to tell me that my house was gone.

Harvey, our unwelcome guest, was gone. We couldn't get out of our front door because of all the metal debris from the roof; we couldn't get out the back door because of the downed trees. Our vehicles were all unreachable or obviously damaged. We couldn't get to dad's house to check on him at first; when we finally hiked over, usually a five-minute walk, it took 30 minutes to get through the debris. Finally, got there and discovered the old truck with a camper shell was still functional. We moved it to the clinic and lived in that camper for the first week. We were lucky. There was a bed and a small generator for a/c. This was more than many people had.

Two days after Harvey, we were out walking the dogs, a three times a day process. Suddenly it was still, no wind, no noise, not even generators, green sky. We were weather traumatized already and wondered where we would go to take shelter. Then we looked down; a hawk had just eaten one of our chickens and was still standing there, not 8 feet away. Absolutely no fear of us. Made the hawk unique in the confrontation; the rest of us were terrified.

I am a Rockport native. I remember Hurricane Celia and the dead horses and cows. Even as a kid, I was interested in animals. I don't remember fear. It was nothing like Harvey; perhaps being older changes perspectives. Now, I know enough to be afraid.

The house was unlivable; the clinic was severely damaged; we couldn't leave because of the animals. When we found the truck with the camper shell, we were grateful. At least we would not be sleeping in a tent.

Every apartment and condo complex in Aransas County was damaged and most were unlivable. Some were low income housing; some were normally filled with Winter Texans starting in October. None would be ready by then. Many apartments had been filled with tenants who worked in the service industries; they cooked, waited tables, worked in WalMart, provided personal

Not Gone With The Wind

care for others. The condos had been filled with tourists who ate the food in restaurants, tipped the wait staff, appreciated WalMart's open 24 hour policy. Housing was going to be a real problem and not just for homeowners. Businesses could not reopen without employees.

I live in Rockport and did not evacuate. I can testify that the first two weeks of the aftermath were worse than the terror during the storm. No power. No water. No sewers. No phone. Trees, or parts of trees, down everywhere. I was luckier than some. We had minimal damage to the house, minimal being a relative term. Our hot water heater was gas, not electric. Eventually, we could take hot showers. Friends came by to visit and enjoy hot water showers.

I remember the throbbing sound of generators for what seemed like weeks. I missed quiet.

I watched in disbelief as the TV showed HEB employees handing out food shortly after the hurricane. I could only imagine what their disaster plan must have included to have services available that quickly in the middle of the devastation that quickly. Then, on the list of open businesses, one of the first to show up was HEB. How did they do that?

"Why did you buy that big welder? You don't know how to weld," I asked my husband some years ago. "Yes, but it has a really big generator." And, sure enough, it did have a really big generator. And we used it 24/7 until the power came on two weeks later.

We got a FEMA motel room in Tilden after 10 days and began driving home to Rockport every other day to try to do things. We were gone for just short of a month.

I came back to town from San Antonio on September 8, saw my church, and cried. I went into the office and saw the black mold on the walls and knew I had to leave. My friend and I came back with the masks and began to try to salvage stuff. If it was moldy, it was thrown out to join the huge trash piles all over town.

The worst part of the hurricane was that we knew that nothing was the same anymore. Our trees looked like plucked chickens, our barn was flattened, our greenhouse folded in on itself ... nothing was the same. I got lost going into town because all my landmarks were gone; there were no streetlights out in the country (or anywhere else). The darkness was overpowering. Going out at night was just impossible. We couldn't even fish ... the piers that we frequented were gone. Nothing was the same ... and it never will be.

Most homes in Holiday Beach had some level of damage if not totalled.

Not Gone With The Wind

Before the hurricane, we had made plans to go to Europe. Without power, without other services in town, we decided to leave on September 4 on the trip planned before Harvey. There was very little that we could do here. We were gone for a month. When we came back, it took six weeks of cutting brush to get the yard back and we had a brush pile the size of the Woman's Club building.

I am a resident of Rockport and I evacuated to my son's house west of Houston. Horrified, I watched on their TV the storm hitting Rockport. I was sure my little house would be gone. My son came with me when I came home to check on my house. When I saw that there was very little damage, I fell to my knees crying. My son thought it was sorrow for the devastation in Rockport; he was wrong. It was joy that my house survived the wrath of Harvey and a generous helping of survivor's guilt. So, I really don't have a story about the hurricane, do I?

September 2 and I am heading to Rockport to help my mom move her horse. Things didn't look too bad in Victoria; Tivoli had downed power lines and power poles snapped off and many damaged buildings. Getting closer to Rockport, I saw that not a single, solitary power line was intact. No one had power. I also began seeing utility crews tasked with the overwhelming responsibility of restoring power to thousands of people. Then there was the airport: airplanes flipped over; roofs of hangers flattened on the aircraft inside. Boat storage facility near Copano Bay completely destroyed. Boats in the roadway; RV's on their sides; entire buildings just gone leaving a concrete slab. I wasn't sure I was going to get to mom's house. Driving over downed power lines, the debris left only one-lane roads at best. A war zone could not look any worse.

No word from any of my friends in our trailer park yet. Then a picture came on Facebook of our trailer. It didn't look too bad ... until the picture of the backside came through. No question about it ... totaled. Two couples who live in the park year round saw pictures of the damage to their units and decided to leave for a two week vacation in Big Bend. Without services available in Rockport, there was no point in hanging around.

When I saw the damage to my RV, I started the process immediately of dealing with the system. My mother says that I spent some part of every day working on my claims, either on-line or in person, for three months. I got my claims through and all settled in 90 days, some sort of a record. I have no idea how my mother would have done by herself without computer skills.

Pop's Tavern & Cafe in Lamar

We had five acres of downed trees, two houses completely hidden by debris, and limited access through the remaining driveways. My son began to work clearing the access; at 96 years old, I was not a lot of help. Who knew how long it would be before we could use the driveway.

Not Gone With The Wind

We constantly watched TV for news of our park; the news was that units left in our park were destroyed. At 80 years of age, the idea of starting over was devastating. Finally, a neighbor got into the park and told us that our unit looked to be in pristine condition. It was a miracle! A few scratches on the window, lost trees, missing shingles on the garage ... didn't need to file a claim. Ours was the only unit in the park without damage.

Several days after landfall, I grew impatient with the warnings to stay out of Rockport. I wanted to see what had happened to my house. So my son and I headed from Corpus to Rockport. As I got close to my home, I began to see the problem. There was so much debris on the road that no car could get through on my normal route. No problem, I would go around the back way. No chance. I finally walked in; my house had no roof ... walls, but no roof. All the windows were intact but water had poured in from the top. All my treasured possessions and the memories attached to them were destroyed.

Finally, satellite and drone pictures began to show up. Why was I having trouble finding our RV park? All that

Home damage in Lamar

was recognizable was Hwy 35 bypass to Corpus, the waterfront and the old HEB store. One park looks much like another, trailers destroyed, trees gone. Hooray, I found it! Despair, my trailer was on its side with no way to tell damage.

We came back from Abilene to check on the house and the cats. Tornado damage to the property but the cats were fine. I have been coming to Rockport since 1984 and have never experienced a storm like Harvey. I will always evacuate in the future.

I had evacuated, the fifth time for me. When I came back on the 8th day after landfall, I had a flashback to my home in Poland during World War II. War zones are similar; no color, debris scattered randomly, vegetation gone, people wandering in a daze. In an instant, I was back in Poland as a child, shivering and panicky. Trauma lasts forever; it returns unexpectedly.

It was so frustrating to be sitting on the overpass with a spotty phone signal talking to FEMA or my insurance company. "Can you hold" after finally getting in ... "Can you attach your information to an email and send it to

Debris pile in front of a home

us" when we had no internet ... "We'll mail you a form" when we had no post office. Some intense disaster training for folks in the call center seems to be indicated.

We headed back to Rockport by way of Portland. After getting the rest of the family settled in my granddaughter's tiny one bedroom house, we started for Rockport. I started crying again at Aransas Pass and didn't really quit for a month. Shadyside Drive wasn't shady; the house had a hole in the roof; who knew what the inside was like.

The damage to our church in the downtown area was immense; the rebuilding job would take months. However, in my mind, a blessing from Harvey was in the destruction of the courthouse. That was an ugly building. I had hoped that it would be replaced for years. Harvey made the decision for us.

The Big Tree SURVIVED! Goose Island State Park

The Woman's Club had minimal damage but members who had evacuated were unable to find any information about its status. Members who did not evacuate took several days before they could get through the debris to come and check on it. By then, the SBA had moved in. No one knows how they got into the building other than someone let them in. Turns out it was probably a Rockport official who, grateful to see an intact building in the center of town, began settling agencies in when they arrived. FEMA followed shortly. Both agencies stayed until the big tent opened across the street. The club was eventually reimbursed for the use of the facilities by the city.

I had come back earlier and found that my park model home and storage shed was now a park model home with a large tree in the bedroom. No storage shed. My business inventory had been in the shed. So, now I am mostly homeless with no business. I am about to become a survival professional.

With the boards off the windows, there was light during the days. The only "entertainment" was watching the people haul off trees ... and more trees ... and more trees. As soon as we would hear the trucks and loaders, the remainder of the neighborhood residents turned out to watch. The sound of chainsaws, the rumble of the trucks and the hum of generators was very comforting to me. Cable addicts were going through withdrawal.

This was the hardest time for me. People in education like answering questions; they don't like saying "I don't know." I spent at least a week saying "I don't know" about everything. Then what little I did know, I couldn't communicate because we had no power, no internet. I had to wait to answer questions until I got back to the hotel in Corpus Christi. I was powerless in so many ways.

Not Gone With The Wind

My husband had come down from Michigan earlier and I arrived on Monday after Harvey. I cried when we came across Hwy 35 and saw the trees bare. We had tree, roof and fence damage but the house was livable. No water, no power and it was HOT! My husband took the remains of the fence and made a shower outside, using well water from the sprinkler system, tannin and all. Then he painted a Texas flag on the shower walls. It became the neighborhood gathering place.

We watched the news from my sister's house in Ft Worth but really weren't prepared. My husband had looked at pictures people sent and decided the house didn't look too bad so he came back a week after Harvey. The trip was bad; flat tires slowed him down. The house was not too badly damaged but ... the refrigerators full of food coupled with the heat made it unlivable. He slept on the porch and helped move trees.

We came back to Rockport down Hwy 188 to Hwy 35 that joins Corpus Christi to Rockport-Fulton-Lamar. On the ocean side, every power pole for miles had a utility truck beside it. The trucks were from everywhere. Where were all these utility workers staying?

I came back about two weeks after Harvey. No power, no water, no phone ... these were all expected. But as I came across 35 from Aransas Pass, I was stunned. It didn't look too bad at first. Then, it was like hitting a wall ... debris everywhere. This I expected ... but no leaves on any trees. No signs. I missed Market street exit and finally turned on Pearl. Everything was grey. It looked like a war zone. I cried. Later, I realized that there was no fishy smell as I remembered from other hurricanes in Mississippi and Louisiana. A small blessing.

About the fourth day, relatives from San Antonio

showed up at my front door. I was amazed. "How did you find me? There are no street signs, no numbers, no landmarks..." I asked. "Easy. Used the GPS. Took me right to you." Who knew?

I am a Winter Texan. There it was, right in my email, a picture of my little blue intact house. One broken palm tree and one broken window. Of course, the flat roof was devoid of the dish and antennas but it was still a roof. How could that be? It was just a little beach house, one block from Little Bay, on concrete blocks, built in the 50's before building codes tried to insure sturdiness. Surely the predicted storm surge would have washed it away. I called my landlord. "Cash my check. I'm coming this winter."

Zelma's place after Harvey

Residents who had not evacuated knew that they were going to live. Residents who had evacuated began to assess their losses. Winter Texans combed YouTube for videos of "their" house or condo.

Technicians worked diligently to restore some bandwith and essential services were improving by August 29th. By August 30th, there was limited bandwith throughout the area. Cell phones work sometimes; internet works sometimes. Without power, residential cable, recharging stations, and other electricity dependent services were unavailable. The sound of generators is reassuring.

Residential trash service begins but it seemed fairly futile, given the volume of debris. There was a Water Boil Advisory while workers assessed the system and checked for leaks. Same for gas and sewers. Residents were advised of the limited capacity of the sewers.

Food, water, and ice was available in several locations. The challenge was to get to it. Volunteers began pouring into the Rockport-Fulton area. Most brought what they needed to survive, including tools, generators, and a place to stay. Many organizations began providing food for workers, volunteers, and residents.

SBA, FEMA, TWIA, TDI open to assist businesses and individuals. SBA and FEMA move to Woman's Club building. As of September 11, 2017, FEMA has distributed $16,000,000 through processed claims.

One of the earliest moves by the city was the decision to establish clear requirements for out-of-area contractors. The city couldn't vouch for the knowledge of the contractors or for the quality of the work but they could make it difficult for scammers to swoop into town and take desperate people's money.  Vetted contractors got stickers for their trucks. Residents were advised to look for the stickers.

The damage to the power grid was complete. AEP thought it might take 30 days to get power to the area since power had to be reconstructed from Corpus Christi to get to Rockport-Fulton peninsula; power had to come

Storm surge and wind damage in Holiday Beach

from Victoria to get to Lamar and Holiday Beach. The area was at the end of the line both from the north and the south. The entire electrical grid for the area had to be rebuilt, starting from Corpus Christi on the south and Victoria on the north. Poles, transformers, all the elements of the grid had to be replaced, a mammoth undertaking. Without power, it would be impossible to provide services to returning evacuees. It was late August, early September; it was hot ... very hot. Air conditioning was not a luxury. Thirty days without power would be another disaster. Thousands of electrical workers from all over came to the area and started working. September 8: 95% of the area was back on power by 10 pm, a remarkable achievement in 16 days from the day power was lost on August 25.

The damage assessments had begun. The obvious damage was to buildings. Miraculously, people who stayed survived. There were no lost lives directly attributable to Harvey.

Over time, various numbers came in. Further inspections by Texas Task Force 1 were made of all facilities in the County to determine livability and continuing operation. News was not good. Generally, 40% of all the buildings in the area were destroyed completely. Another 35% were uninhabitable and would need to be rebuilt. In all, 96% of the buildings in Aransas County were damaged.

- Schools: All buildings were damaged or partially destroyed. No estimate when school would resume.
- Public Buildings: Aransas County Courthouse was destroyed and would have to be demolished.
- The Pavilions on Rockport Beach were damaged and would have to be rebuilt.
- Paws and Taws, the Fulton Convention Center, was destroyed and would have to be demolished.
- Public Parks: All were damaged, including the ball fields.
- Fulton Mansion: Damaged.
- Rockport Center for the Arts: Heavily Damaged, will

Quick Mart and Laundromat at Market and Magnolia, Rockport

be demolished.
- Rockport Aquarium: Demolished.
- Rockport, Fulton and Cove Harbors and Blue Wave Beach: Filled with debris, most structures damaged.
- Fishing Piers: Damaged, unusable.
- Bay Education Center: Damaged, unusable.
- Texas Maritime Museum: Damaged, repairable.
- Big Blue Crab: Gone.
- Aransas Wildlife Refuge: took the brunt of the 12.5 foot storm surge.
- Rockport Cultural Arts District: damaged, many buildings gone.
- Churches: the majority sustained major damage to their buildings.
- Businesses: Very few could immediately reopen.
- Water and sewer: damaged, repair a priority.
- Big Tree: survived with damage but was not uprooted.

City and county employees were affected by Harvey just like everyone else. Over 40 of the 128 employees were homeless. Most had evacuated their families while they stayed. And yet, they all showed up, working 12 hours on and 12 hours off for weeks. They did what needed to be done, regardless of their job description.

Mosquito sighted the size of a hummingbird ... nightly spraying will continue. Cranky rattlesnakes forcibly evacuated from St. Joe's Island were reported. Get a tetanus shot; wear protective clothing to work in clean-up; plan for flat tires.

Mail delivery will be attempted if a mailbox is still standing.

Texas A&M Forestry Service will evaluate trees and advise about the next steps.

Major debris pickup to clean up roads starts on September 5 with up to 60 trucks, processing 25,000 tons of debris daily. As roads are cleared, major debris pickup for residents begins. First to be picked up are limbs and tree debris because of their high flammability. As of September 14, 2017, over 100,000 cubic yards of debris have been removed. As of September 20, 217,691 cubic yards of debris removed, not counting TxDOT efforts on roads. As of September 27, 2017 395,549 cubic yards of debris removed.

September 6: The first post-Harvey print edition of the Rockport Pilot is available, a remarkable feat since there is still no power.

September 9: Curfew changed to 10 pm to 6 am. School classes will resume in 30 days.

Leaning power lines and poles south of Rockport along Hwy 35 Business

Street lights were possible now that the power was on. Street lights were damaged by Harvey and would have to be replaced before the lights could come back even with the power available. The big trash trucks were very tall ... with tall booms above the trucks ... tall enough to take out the few remaining traffic lights.

School Administrators (Superintendent) had the first task; the community wanted information about the schools. Basic questions around when, where, how were asked over and over. It was frustrating for the first week because the information just did not exist, especially the when question. The only habitable school building was the Rockport School, built in 1933. Administration moved in with the Information Technology staff and began to get information out, through the internet, through Facebook. While there was generator power to send out information from the district, there was little or no power on the

Salt Grass Landing Apartments damage

receiving end for the people still in Rockport. At least the people who had evacuated could get the news. Still kept getting lots of questions. Life improved dramatically when the power came on.

South Rockport along Hwy 35 Business

COPANO BAY AND KEY ALLEGRO

I live on Copano Cove. The eye passed directly over my house, according to Google Maps. The calm lasted about 2 ½ hours and I decided to take the dogs outside. The front side of the hurricane had been bad and the dogs showed no desire to go back out again. I think they knew that the worst was still to come.

In Austin, my son and I are watching the Weather Channel as Harvey comes ashore. Suddenly my home security system in Key Allegro in Rockport begins to go off. A window was breached. Twenty minutes later, the door was breached. Then silence.

I had no house to return to ... and I brought nothing to survive with me. I had packed for two days. Yet my car was intact; I had some minimal paperwork; I had insurance. And my next door neighbor was a builder who had already offered to help me rebuild. And my son and grandson wanted me to come live with them in Victoria. While I grieved for my house and all its memories, I knew that I was so fortunate. I could have chosen to stay in my Key Allegro house during Harvey. The house was completely destroyed.

Fence and home damages in Copano Village

Not Gone With The Wind

I evacuated from my condo in Allegro North but came back on Monday. My home was unlivable. I am a realtor and couldn't stay away from my office. It was damaged, dark, and moldy but somehow, I was comforted there. I saw a woman outside looking over toward my condos and I asked her if she was from TWIA (Texas Wind Insurance Agency). No, from SBA, assessing damage. To my horror, I burst into tears in front of a total stranger. She wrapped me in a big hug and let me cry. She told me that it would be OK; it would take time. I still cry unexpectedly but I know that we will survive. Sometimes, it just takes a hug.

We saw the videos. We knew the damage on Copano Bay was extensive. We decided a pop-up trailer and a generator would be a good plan when we went back.

Our house on Copano Bay was built to Florida hurricane standards and then beefed up. Every place that a hurricane strap could be placed, it had been. The main part of the house had been built on piers. We didn't evacuate for health reasons but we felt safe. And we were. But we experienced all of Harvey. The eye took two and a half hours to go over our house; the winds and then the silence were terrifying. And when the dirty side of the hurricane started to pass over, the wind noise changed dramatically. I could hear the sounds of the tornados to the north of us, in Bayside. Our house had minimal damage but houses next door and two doors down had extensive damage, primarily on the inside. The randomness of the damage was mystifying.

Overheard and not verified: Everything I owned was out in Copano Bay, including me. I clutched a pile of debris that used to be my dock and prayed. The wind howled and seemed to come from every direction. Absolute darkness in the middle of the night. The water wasn't deep enough to drown me but I couldn't keep my footing. Finally, it seemed to lessen and I crawled out of the water onto the debris. It shifted and I looked to my left. Eyes. Not good. Alligator eyes. Really not good. Truce. We shared my dock until the wind dropped. He left first.

Several people reported that Harvey emptied Copano Bay, just sucked the water away from the shore.... but then refilled it with a vengeance. Others watched as water drained away from Mustang Island and then poured back over the dunes. If your house had a twelve foot elevation, you would be fine. A six foot elevation.... you got over six feet of water in your lower level.

We weren't leaving. We had worked for six years on our house in Copano Heights, just moved in, and we believed it would withstand a hurricane. However, we needed to get my elderly parents to safety so we went

Positive Attitudes Go a Long Way

Not Gone With The Wind

Key Allegro home after Harvey

to Beeville with them. We watched the hurricane hit Rockport, followed the eye as it passed over our house and began to see the pictures of destruction. I cried but my husband held me and said that we would get through this together. After all, it was only a house. He was right and we did get through it. The house survived with some water damage ... and trees were damaged. We would always know that the house we built to withstand a hurricane did just that.

My house on Copano Bay was still standing...sort of. I started my TWIA/FEMA/Flood Insurance odyssey. I learned that if you have private insurance, you may not be eligible for most forms of assistance. However, TWIA was formed to handle wind damage and most private insurance companies send wind claims to TWIA. The first inspection verdict: total loss. The saga continues.

I feed birds on Key Allegro. I came back and there were no birds ... no sparrows, not even any gulls. I put food out but no one came. Then one day, a single dove showed up. I worried. She was alone. I put out more food to help her out. A true lonesome dove. I think that she and I were successful. I saw two doves on the feeder.

Assessments were in and several different ones agreed that 56% of the buildings around Copano Bay and in Key Allegro were destroyed. Both areas were chosen by builders and residents for their proximity to the water for water sports and for the fishing. Key Allegro, where land was limited, had small lots, many with large houses. Other owners there had small lots and built their houses on piers overhanging the Aransas Bay. The early pictures after Harvey, tending toward the dramatic, featured Key Allegro houses slumping into the water when dislodged from their supports. Anyone looking at Key Allegro closely could see the vulnerability. Perhaps that is why there is a mandatory evacuation when a hurricane threatens.

Key Allegro home from the canal

Not Gone With The Wind

Copano Bay, on the northern side of the Live Oak peninsula, has a different feel. In some areas, Copano Ridge for example, there are small lots with bay access and long fishing piers or canals. In other areas, there are large lots and large houses, some with piers and others with views. For the most part, the lots around Copano Bay are real land. Key Allegro is created land in many cases with houses built on fill sand dredged and dumped on the existing underwater land.

Both Copano Bay and Key Allegro have a history going back to the Karankawa tribe that had to have been the early Winter Texans. They came to the coast for the abundant seafood and mild weather. Their version of carry-out differed from ours but the principle was the same. Early settlers were willing to fight the vicious brush and settled in various places around Copano Bay. Entrepreneurs tried to develop Copano Bay as a deep-water port starting in the 1840's but events always defeated them. The Civil War took a toll. They were gaining on the project in the 1900's until the 1919 Hurricane dumped sand in Copano and the work to dredge the bay halted progress. Then the King Ranch began negotiating for Corpus Christi Bay to be developed into the deepwater port on the Gulf Coast and they won. Copano Bay became a backwater.

A very large backwater, however, with excellent

Marina on Key Allegro

fishing. Fishermen began to arrive and built fishing camps ... small, relatively primitive, cabins. Some of the early developments in the area had more in common with the fishing camps than with the later, larger houses. The Copano Bay area developments often were in Aransas County, not in Rockport or Fulton, and residents preferred to remain in the county and fought against annexation. With the hurricane, came a price. Some of the heaviest damage happened in the county and the county appeared to have fewer resources to deal with the devastation than did the urban areas.

Key Allegro began to develop much later, in the 1960's. Carl Kreuger, Jr bought Frandolig Point in 1961 from the Aransas County Navigation District, planning a resort community with 1000 homes, a golf course, and a marina. The resort community for weekenders and tourists became an affluent community of second-home owners and permanent residents. By the mid 1990's, the land was built out and population stabilized at 600. Then

Relocating a surviver from Copano Ridge home

Not Gone With The Wind

prospective owners began buying the older beach cottages, tearing them down, and building newer, larger homes. Key Allegro's attractions, access to big water, fishing and water sports, were also points of vulnerability in a hurricane.

Harvey devastated both areas. The eye hovered over Copano, taking two and a half hours to pass over a single spot. The high winds, up to 228 mph, in the eye wall had plenty of time to grind away at the structures. The mesovortices, like tornados to mid-westerners, dropped down randomly, destroying one house and leaving the next untouched. In both areas, relatively new structures, built to contemporary hurricane codes, fared better than older ones in most cases. But not always ... a smaller, older, home on a slab instead of piers might have survived while a newer unit on piers that the water got in when the roof was damaged, was destroyed.

Some Copano and Key Allegro residents are taking their insurance money if there was any and leaving the area; others want to rebuild what they had; still others are rebuilding to new hurricane codes. But neither Copano Bay nor Aransas Bay care; their broad expanses will survive.

COORDINATION

Like many other Winter Texans, I read every one of the daily bulletins posted online by the Mayor of Rockport. We couldn't contact friends here directly, since there was no power, but we were able to follow what was happening thanks to the Mayor's remarkable coordination of relief efforts and information dissemination. We decided immediately that we would return this winter if we possibly could, and do our part to keep the tourist economy alive.

The letters were our only way of communicating directly with our residents and then only with residents who had evacuated. No power, no internet, no cell phone service meant that residents who stayed were isolated. Although I sent the first letters starting right after Harvey left, by September 7 we wanted everyone to know that the one city, one town and one county spoke with One Voice. We would tell one story.

As a Winter Texan, I became an obsessive reader of Mayor Wax's letters and watcher of YouTube. My brain knew about the devastation but my emotions didn't want to admit that the lovely town I loved might not recover.

It seemed to me that coordination on a local level was much more effective than the coordination at a state and federal level. All the frogs were in a much smaller pond. Perhaps it was because assistance was on a very individual level; there were fewer steps to navigate for those who needed help. Also, the volunteers who poured into the area were not focused on fraud prevention, hence less paperwork. In addition, much of the volunteer work came to be coordinated by the local churches. These churches were used to doing mission work and knew the community well. Local coordination was not perfect but the use of remaining community resources allowed for more to be done with less.

A talented athlete or dancer or roofer is a marvel to watch. Somehow, the individual is aware of all the parts of the body and, through hours of practice, has learned to function in ways that most of us cannot imagine. With luck, the individual has dropped the pass or forgotten the steps or lost the hammer during practice. With even more luck, no one saw it happen. Coordination requires talent but also practice. It is possible to practice for a football game, a square dance, a job on a very tall building. Practice for a hurricane ... it is all dry runs for the local coordinators who don't remember Beulah or Carla. They hope that, if the performance is flawed, no one will ever see it.

As a Winter Texan, I watched compulsively from a distance. I had the feeling of watching a carefully choreographed square dance and hoped I wasn't watching if someone missed a step. The number of participants in this dance were substantial; the acronyms alone used nearly every letter in the alphabet. SBA, FEMA, HUD, CDBG, CBDRG, LTR, VRC, TWIA ... mind boggling. Groups from every level of government, federal, state, local, were all in town ... at the same time ... all with agendas ... all needing a place to work ... Harvey wasn't the only swirling, windy hurricane that the town had to deal with. And in the eye of this hurricane were the local Rockport-Fulton-Aransas County officials, Mayor Wax of Rockport, Mayor Kendrick of Fulton, and Judge Mills of Aransas County. They gave the impression to distant observers of the calm in the eye of the official hurricane. I think that was part of the dance.

One of the early moves that was crucial was the notion that the three officials spoke with one voice. No chance to set up a situation where the officials were pitted against each other in the public mind. Undoubtedly, there were disagreements among themselves but in the end, there was one dance caller, one voice. No report surfaced of bloodshed and the square dance continued.

Coaches have game plans, playwrights have scripts, Harvey had daily letters. The early letters were primarily seen by evacuees and Winter Texans since the folks that stayed were without power, internet, or time to do much but survive. They did set the dance steps for the evacuees who were coming back. People were warned about curfews, debris in the roads, lack of services, snakes, mosquitoes. Returning residents knew that they had to bring everything with them or suffer the consequences. The letters provided directions ... ignored by some as always ... and a sense that someone was in control and knew what they were doing. In the old swamp and alligators saying, people felt that someone was working on their alligators. And the square dance continued.

Politics in Texas are brutal; the dance is filled with changing partners, backsteps, sidesteps. When Governor Abbott arrived, he fit into the dance as though he had practiced with the group. He mourned, he encouraged, he promised money and he delivered trash trucks. Fantastic! Some political figures who promise more than they deliver are referred to, in the Texas lingo, as all hat and no cattle. When it came to Harvey's debris leftovers, Governor Abbott had hat and cattle.

The dance continued with stomping and kicking, steps and missteps, handshakes, hand offs, and the usual quota of inflated egos that come with government. Still the dance as a whole moved slowly forward. But many elected officials said that if they knew then what they know now, they would never have run for office. A Category 4 Hurricane is just not in the usual job description. In addition, the salary of an elected official in Aransas County would barely cover a fancy cup of coffee a day for a month.

St. Peters Catholic Church

Church Unlimited in Downtown Rockport

CHURCHES

Holy Cross Evangelical Lutheran Church and all its members were hit hard by Harvey. The church, parsonage, and the trees were heavily damaged. As the Windstorm Adjuster said, "this place looks totaled." The steeple blew off and has never been found. The wind blew over the granite columbarium. As overwhelming as the damage was, the support received by the church and its members was just as overwhelming. First was the offer of a small, old, empty concrete building that had survived for worship. Next was the support from other congregations and the synod, both money and goods as well as volunteer services. Groups of volunteers came, some staying a week and others staying for several weeks. Boxes of goods arrived; checks came in the mail tagged REBUILD; WalMart gift cards came from a congregation in San Antonio. We are blessed.

St. Peters Catholic Church, a Vietnamese congregation, was heavily damaged. Knights of Columbus came to help. The congregation is much more resilient than their building.

Sacred Heart Catholic Church was heavily damaged, particularly the parish hall, the office and the school. The area above the offices where the nuns had lived was gone. Although I was angry when the new jail was built directly across the street, I was amazed to see that it was that sturdy jail that probably prevented further damage to the narthex. Fortunately, the church had good insurance.

My church, Church of Jesus Christ of Latter Day Saints, sustained very little damage. It was open to everyone as a refuge during the hurricane and after as well. The Bishop was here and helped the church provide relief for

Not Gone With The Wind

anyone who needed it. Church members worked together to help clean up trees for members and non-members.

Harvey changed things. We have always been an open church but now on Sundays, there is a whole new group of people attending worship each week. The volunteers, First Responders, workers ... they are from all over. We have a chance, as a congregation, to say thank you.

As a Winter Texan, we love Rockport. We attend a small church with a group of friends that we visit with each year. We called Marsha, a friend who evacuated, and she said she was not sure what would happen to the church after Harvey. Then her phone number no longer worked; after our arrival, we saw that the church was no longer in its place in the store front. We were sad to hear that the church had disbanded. Then, I saw Marsha in HEB. The church was meeting in the pastor's home. We reconnected and all is well. However, there are only half the number attending that there were before Harvey.

St. Peters Catholic Church

The pastor said that the landlord had raised the rent substantially after repairing the hurricane damage, a common story. Our RV park rates went up also but we plan to keep returning to our favorite winter getaway in sunny, warm, friendly Rockport, Texas.

My mother and I evacuated but because of the short notice, we just threw stuff in the car and had to leave the RV in the park. We had two or three changes of clothing, family pictures, some paperwork and very little else. We were on the road when I remembered that I had not gotten my favorite picture of Jesus out of the RV. Mom said that we left him in charge of the RV. When we came back, the front of the RV had blown off the jacks and the rig was tilted to the front. Inside, Jesus had fallen off the wall and the water that had gotten in flowed away from the picture toward the front of the RV. Most of the RV was dry.

On Thursday the 24th, I was heading out of town. My husband refused to leave for fear of looters. There wasn't enough time to put up plywood. I was frightened ... of the storm, of the idea of starting over, of the potential losses. I chose to go to each room in my house and sprinkle holy water and ask God to bless and protect my house and the people who lived in it. With nothing more that I could do, I left. On Saturday morning, I got word from my husband that he was alive. I was grateful. But what about my house? I came back on September 8th and was awed. My house was untouched. The only damage was to our freestanding garage. I hadn't thought to ask protection for the garage. Even more amazing, the insurance claim went through quickly and there was enough money to fix the damage to the garage and to fix damage to the siding that was there before Harvey. I will never underestimate the power of intentional prayer. However, I do think that I should have tried to go by the church building before leaving town.

Not Gone With The Wind

Rockport-Fulton-Lamar was a fishing area for the Karankawa Indians from the beginning. Then came settlers and, after the Civil War, a port for the meat packing industry, followed by fishing and shipbuilding. Later, artists came for the beauty. But from the beginning of the settlements, there were churches. Stella Maris, Star of the Sea, a Catholic chapel in Lamar was completed in 1858, project of Irish immigrant James W. Byrne. Built of shellcrete, it is still standing despite Harvey's worst.

The same cannot be said of the many other churches in the area. Most had major damage. And yet ... and yet ... None of my storytellers referred to their church in the past tense. It was as though a favorite tool had been damaged. The church, as a building, was not The Church. Life and the missions continued.

Despite extensive damage to their buildings, the churches proved to be much more than buildings. The First Baptist Church has served as the volunteer center. Peace Lutheran Church opened the church almost immediately, serving as a distribution center for donations and feeding volunteer workers. Coastal Oaks Baptist Church had a lesser amount of damage of the churches in the area. The church gym was used as a donation center with truckloads of donations being unloaded and people coming in for help. The Pastor had damage to his home but volunteers came in to help rebuild. As was true in many cases, members worked at the church first instead of their homes. Every congregation has a story ... of mission, of sacrifice, of dedication, of generosity. Without the churches, Harvey's picture would have been much darker.

THE AFTERMATH: POWER

September 10-October 11, 2017

Aransas County

The senior athletes will never forget their senior year. Normal ... disaster ... displacement ... powerlessness ... nothing was normal again. Except the coaches. They were still there. Still demanding. Still work oriented. Providing structure to the days. Work out first, then community service. The work was not academic ... hauling brush and debris ... helping folk who needed help ... being needed. The feeling of being in control of at least one part of their situation was therapeutic; the usefulness of their youth and strength was invigorating. They learned that they could make change happen. They had power and it wasn't just on the sports fields.

When the power came back on, our son was able to get in and check on our home. Only minor damage! Lots of damage In the rest of the park and it would take work to get things livable.

All the nursing homes, assisted living facilities, hospital rooms in Aransas County were gone. Their occupants had been evacuated, often with the staff and nurses of the facility. The systems in the surrounding area were strained by the evacuees. The family caregivers were strained too. To visit an evacuee meant a substantial drive roughly scheduled around contractors who might be there ... or might not. The facilities where their folk had ended up often were not set up to deal with the problems that their incoming clients had. Those facilities had empty beds but often limited staff. Nothing was the same; it would be months before facilities closer to home would reopen.

I feed the hummingbirds and am involved in the Hummerbirds festival every year the third week in September. Rockport is a major stop on the migration path of these little birds and residents put out feeders all over Rockport when it is time for them to come through. The migration starts around the middle of August and tapers off in mid-October. The birds didn't get the notice; Harvey had cancelled the Hummerbird festival. Not only did their usual stopping place look different, there were no feeders, no flowers, no vegetation. No residents to fill the feeders. I came out one morning I came out and found a little guy, feet locked around a branch, dead, probably of starvation. I had been so busy with personal survival that I forgot that hummingbirds were coming through. Sugar was in short supply so I sent word to relatives to stock up for me. I started with two feeders and eventually worked up to 10 feeders on the porch. I filled them over and over and over....no more dead birds.

Rental property is a problem. FEMA has few resources for landlords. But often, the cost of the new roof and other repairs is more than the building is worth. Yet, the tenants have nowhere else to live. Both tenant and landlord are trapped.

I was worried. As there was progress in the area in clearing out debris and assessing damage, it became clear that most of the people providing services in the area had lost their homes and moved out of the area. Some evacuated out of the area, enrolled their kids in school in the new area, and got jobs there. Others would have come back to their jobs if there had been a place to live. Others had housing of sorts but ... no child care was available in the area. All the preschools that had been located in churches were closed because the facilities were damaged. The Aransas County Independent School District was closed. Unless there was a local grandmother, the workers couldn't work because there was no child care. It became a vicious circle: no restaurant could reopen without cooks and servers; no one could commute from housing in Corpus Christi for a service job income; without childcare, no one could take a job, no matter what the pay was. Since the Rockport

Damaged airplane in a damaged hanger at the Airport

Multiple downtown businesses

area depends on tourist income, it showed signs of being a bad winter.

Facilitate communication ... one of the jobs of the library. But we were in the same shape as the other county agencies. No power, no internet, no cell phone service. Unless a library patron was standing right in front of us, we could do nothing. In fact, we weren't sure we even had a building left until I got back to town to find that, yes indeed, the library survived. And was now occupied by multiple agencies, including Fish and Wildlife and was papered with maps. Agencies used any building that survived as a central point for their projects. Agencies like Fish and Wildlife stayed until mid September.
The library was back in the business of facilitating communication.

One day, a group from FEMA and Homeland Security came in to the Woman's Club and announced that they needed the space and that the Woman's Club needed to evict the current tenants by the next morning. They couldn't say how long they would need the space but the impression was that this group was part of a long term recovery team. There was some confusion since one of the current occupants was FEMA. They also thought that there would be no charge for the use of the space. Since the Woman's Club owns and maintains their building, revenue is crucial. After the Woman's Club treasurer produced spreadsheets and informed the group about the monthly income for events hosted, the FEMA group decided to look elsewhere for free space rather than have to reimburse the club for lost revenue. The group may have misjudged the Woman's Club; they may have thought that this was a group of ladies who would be impressed by officialdom and who could be intimidated into complying by Homeland Security. The club realized that as citizens, they had some power over property. A learning opportunity for all involved.

After being out of our home for almost a month, we came home. My husband had a stroke just four days after we returned home.

Con artists descended almost immediately. My husband came back early and noticed that the neighbor had already had his roof replaced. It looked pretty good so

Collapsed home in Aransas County

Stella Maris, Star of the Sea, a Catholic chapel in Lamar

he asked who had done the work so quickly. Neighbor said that the insurance agent recommended him. Called the guy and a salesman came to give a quote, assuring him that they would do the work for the amount of the insurance. Husband signed the contract but the salesman didn't leave a copy, said would send one by email. Email finally arrived and it looked different from what husband remembered. After endless attempts to contact the company, some changes were made. One was that husband wasn't ready for roofers yet because the fence was being fixed. He would call when ready for shingles to be delivered. Four weeks passed, no calls from either party and the shingles showed up, unexpectedly. He refused delivery and was told there would be a 25% restocking fee, which he refused to pay. He began to wonder so checked to see if building permit had been filed. No. Checked on neighbor's address. No building permit there either. The contract was void and neighbor's roof had to be removed at the roofer's expense and reinstalled after a permit filed.

Our church kitchen was destroyed; the parish hall was gone. We had a problem. There was no place to hold funeral dinners. We began limiting the number of people we could provide for. I started carrying all the supplies in my car. The Woman's Club was out of creamer? No problem, I had it my trunk.

When I came back from San Antonio where we evacuated, my wife looked at Rockport and said that I needed to allot more time for each appointment in my vision practice. I didn't understand at first; then I knew that she had been right. Everyone needed to talk. Even now, months after Harvey, I still allot more time for each appointment. It seems important.

There was no color when I got back. No leaves on the

trees; leaves on the ground were brown; live oaks were grey; debris was colorless. I loved the bright lime green piece of clothing ... shorts or swim suit ... in the trees on the back road to WalMart. It was there for weeks, the only bright sight in the grey.

I am a Rockport native who evacuated. My rental house was unlivable when I came back and my landlord is in London ... England, that is. Not a guarantee of prompt action. My recommendation: Make good friends as you live your life. You never know when you will need help. I have been "homeless" for four months, living with a succession of friends. I am now settled in with my

Debris and damaged home in Fulton

grandson, making the supreme sacrifice of caring for my great-grandkids. I can't imagine my life after Harvey without my friends and family.

What to do? Our winter home was gone. Should we take this opportunity to go somewhere else? We thought about Arizona, and Florida, and other places in Texas. Then a message came; a model in our park similar to ours that we had always admired was going to come on the market. No hesitation...we bought it. We would deal with FEMA and TWIA after we got home to Rockport. Another text message: a friend lost her home and couldn't get another until settlements came in. Our friend is now living in our new home; we pulled the fifth wheel trailer from Canada and parked in the spot vacated by our destroyed trailer. We're back home in Rockport.

Saltwater Pavilion at Rockport Beach Park

We came back after the power came on and our park model home was only moderately damaged ... certainly livable. Minor repairs and we were good to go. Our son, who had checked on the unit, noticed that none of the permanent sheds near the park models appeared to have any damage. How the trees that fell missed them all and most of the trailers was astonishing. The community building was another story. It had appeared very sturdy and may have been the community shelter in case of storm; it is still not completely open. Harvey's winds were unpredictable.

Coming back, Rockport looked like there had been a forest fire. No leaves, only the grey sticks of the trees standing. And yet, within a very short period, the trees began to bud ... in September. It was amazing.

Good news: I saw no looters. Other news: Continued dealing with TWIA ... continued dealing with TWIA ... more inspections ... more reviews. I was tempted to ask the adjustor if his mother knew how he earned his living. Discretion prevailed.

Powerless. I was powerless to fix my house; powerless to make things move faster; powerless to deal with the whole Harvey situation. So I did what any clear thinking hurricane victim would do ... left the country. I went to Spain, where I had lived for a time. It was a good decision because it moved me beyond the feeling of hurricane-induced paralysis. Law of Unintended Consequences came into full play ... I broke my leg. Life got more complicated.

Home demolition on Key Allegro.

Many Winter Texans who had RV's or trailers came earlier than usual to their parks. It was just too hard to stay away from a place that we loved. Some of us came to assess damage to our rigs; others came to help the rebuilding process. As a general rule, motor homes stayed upright with damage; travel trailers ended up on their tongues with damage; fifth wheels went over with damage. It was very unusual for a rig to be undamaged.

Harvey had a way of unseating fence sitters. People who had thought of fixing parts of a home that were not working well ... plumbing, for example ... were left with an entire house being bulldozed. No more procrastinating, build a new house or leave town. Other people who had been urged by children to move to another town found themselves in that town and stayed. Restaurant owners who had intended to upgrade the restaurant kitchen when life slowed down a bit were forced to replace the kitchen and most of the rest of the building if they wanted to reopen. Other restaurant owners whose establishments would best be described as quaint (old), picturesque (fish on the wall, watch your step signs) with ambience (old furniture, essence of fish) were unfixable. Construction demolition projects that had been on hold were assisted by Harvey ... large holes in walls, no roof ... that tended to force the issue. People

Palm trees down in Copano Ridge

who once had options found them more limited than they thought. Many decisions to be made in a limited period of time. Stress.

While evacuated at the third hotel, I was finally going to have a lower floor. I had been carrying my fat 14 year old dog up and down the stairs. Happily, I texted my family "Hallelujah, I have a first floor room so I don't have to carry Porko up and down the stairs. It's killing me!" Unfortunately, the spell checker changed Porko to Porno. Technology is our friend ... ?

The house didn't look too bad on the outside; outside staircase gone, deck damaged, some windows broken. We couldn't get inside easily but it didn't look like water had gotten in. The biggest problem were the trees. The house wasn't accessible because the driveway was blocked by all the debris in the street. The spot designated to deposit the debris was soon overwhelmed. Mount TxDOT, soon to rival Mount Everest, was created in the median of the highway bypass to Corpus Christi. The city/county/state effort to haul debris was outstanding. It had to be a priority; otherwise, Aransas County was paralyzed.

I have a souvenir of Harvey. Shortly after moving home, I noticed a strange thing in my garage. There was an odd tannish brown pile, pyramid shaped, in the middle of the floor. It looked like a very tidy pile of sand except it was not Rockport sand. Sand here is uniformly grey, sort of oyster shell color. This was brown and rusty and golden and tan rounded pellets ... foreign sand. It remained, unchanging, for several months until I scooped it up and put it in a jar. I decided that this was ground up Harvey with bits of roof, and metal, and plywood and live oak in it, heavier than normal Rockport sand, because it was so much more than sand.

My assisted living facility for rehab in Rockport was gone but I wanted to leave the facility in Austin that I had been evacuated to. I had no money, no credit card, no checkbook ... everything like that was in my house. I hoped that all would have survived. So I called the Rockport-Fulton Chamber of Commerce and they sent me a bus ticket and I headed home. I found that the people who were going to board up my house had found it too complicated and did not do anything; the house was severely damaged.

These kids will think that they are pro players was my first thought. The University Interscholastic League said kids could play for their original school. No classes, just play football or volleyball. UIL's first answer to displaced students lacked practicality, especially since I couldn't predict when school would reopen. Gregory-Portland school systems took 1400 of our kids so they could continue to attend school when we were closed; Sinton had another 200. Others were scattered in districts all over. We told parents to enroll their students wherever they ended up finding a place to live. But then there

Collapsed apartment complex

were the athletes ... who were they going to play for? They all wanted to be Pirates ... Rockport-Fulton Pirates to be exact. I had the University Interscholastic League on speed dial. The next ruling was that students had to play where they were attending. Didn't fly. Kids stopped attending their new school or would never enroll. They would wait for Rockport Fulton to reopen, however long it took, and play as RF Pirates. They began coming on campus to work out on their own. The football coach and the other coaches noticed and began meeting them. They allowed them to work out but the Athletic Director and staff sent them into the community in work squads to do recovery work. The young coaches organized the teams; the Athletic Director's wife organized the tasks. This went on for several weeks while administrators tried to figure out how to get students back in classes and allow them to play for the Pirates. As it was, they were not in classes. Amazing how idle students force change quickly in institutions not noted for flexibility and speed. New ruling: Students could play for Rockport-Fulton if they chose but they had to be attending classes somewhere in order to do so. The first football game was in

Debris Pile AGAIN

Sinton on September 8, long before our schools reopened.

FEMA became a gathering place. The couple in front of me were frustrated. Everything they owned was out in Copano Bay ... the trailer, the shed, the porch, their boat, one of their cars ... all in the Bay. The FEMA person on the phone that they talked to told them that they needed to have the deed to their trailer to file papers. The deed was in the trailer ... in the bay. So, they were told that they needed to get to their city hall to get a copy of the deed. Of course, the city hall was destroyed. No copy of the deed. Then they were told that they had 60 days to get their stuff out of the bay. I left before I heard the outcome. Both sides were frustrated, one that their regulations didn't cover the situation; the other that the regulations couldn't be followed. I suspect that this was not the first time or the last for this type of problem.

Gas Station in Lamar at Hwy 35 and Park Road 13

Not Gone With The Wind

The power was back on, still a boil order for water. Utility workers were checking every system for leaks, water, sewer, gas. More people were coming back; more people found themselves newly homeless.

Mail service had to rebuild along with the utilities. Immediately after the storm, all services were performed out of Corpus Christi. Drivers brought the mail to Rockport from Corpus Christi; the drivers were not from the area and often were unable to find addresses to deliver the mail because all the street signs were down, not to mention house numbers or whole houses missing. So the mail went back to Corpus Christi since there was no functional post office in Rockport or Fulton.

The water damage was not from flooding near Aransas Bay; it was from holes in the roof from the wind. Not so in Copano Bay; storm surge was a problem there The wind damage was everywhere ... sort of. The randomness of the absolute damage was mystifying. One house completely shattered; the next house relatively intact. Older structures suffered more damage; newer structures were not immune though. The meteorologists talked about mesovortices in the eye wall. Winter Texans from the Midwest recognized the signs of tornadoes. The fact that Harvey stayed in the area for so long ... almost 13 hours over Rockport ... allowed the hurricane force winds to just grind away at buildings, trees, power poles, fences, more trees, homes.

Not surprising then that many residents lost not only their homes but their businesses. It was good that SBA came in early. Processes are tedious but SBA made low interest loans available quickly. Unfortunately, many people didn't understand that the SBA is a bank ... making loans. No job, no loan was still the rule of thumb.

THE AFTERMATH: POWER

The "Claw" trucks that picked up DEBRIS

After power was restored, bandwidth was better; water, sewer, and gas were safe; the overwhelming task was the debris. Many of the trees that were destroyed were the old live oaks, massive trunks, outstretched branches, shallow root structure. Houses in Rockport are built around the oaks and often very close to them. A two-hundred-year-old live oak with a twelve-foot circumference is not at all unusual. The trees were often uprooted and then dumped on the house, resulting in debris from the tree and from the house. People who lived on acreage came back to ... to ... Where was the house? So many trees, large and small, were uprooted or sheared off that the house was no longer visible or accessible.

Residential trash was restored first but couldn't deal with the volume. Pleas went to the governor for more trash haulers and the trucks arrived. Double trucks with

Not Gone With The Wind

claw lifters to fill both open truck boxes ... huge trucks ... tall trucks ... tall enough to take out the few remaining traffic lights.

The transfer station was overwhelmed early; land out by the airport was made available; it was not enough space either. So, Mount Harvey, aka Mount TxDOT, was created. A transfer station was established in the median of Hy35. Eventually 3.1 million cubic yards of debris was hauled, enough to cover over a mile of the median.

People seeing it couldn't decide how to feel ... angry at a dump in the middle of the road; horrified at the sight of all that debris; grateful that all that stuff was no longer in their front yard; proud of the visible progress being made.

Gradually, postal services moved to Aransas Pass. Post office boxes were re-established in Rockport in a double wide trailer in the parking lot; packages were available in tents and wagons, also in the parking lot.

The criteria to reopen the schools came to be pretty basic. At least one kitchen that could prepare meals and distribute to the other buildings. Power ... without air conditioning, the schools could not reopen. Water ... obvious. Sewer ... even more obvious. Rooms somewhere to put students and teachers ... probably not where they

The start of the debris pile in the median of Hwy 35 Bypass.

were before Harvey. Since our student count would be down from pre-Harvey levels, reopening did not seem out of reach.

Schools, in many communities, are the center of activity, of pride, of tradition. It is particularly damaging when an event like Harvey seems to attack the schools. But schools are part of a network, both in their own towns and in their states. Donations of money, goods, and services began to pour in. Surplus furniture from a district near Dallas, surplus technology from other districts, Pirate t-shirts sold in Lubbock-Cooper, a different Pirate school district, band instruments, sports equipment. No one could donate a new gym but insurance covers buildings. The other donations covered the feelings of isolation. Never any question ... the schools will reopen. The rebuilding ... that will take longer.

When digital modes fail, paper and ink shine. The Rockport Pilot, despite damage to the building, put out the first post-Harvey print edition on September 6, 2017. Contrary to the coverage of Houston in national papers, the Rockport Pilot reported about Aransas County, Rockport, Fulton, Lamar, and Holiday Beach.

The generosity of volunteers with free food was amazing.

- Houston ... not so much.
- Austin ... only as the actions of the government impacted this area.
- Washington, D.C ... is that where FEMA comes from?

The paper reported on the issues that their constituency wanted to know about. The editorial content remained civil and calm and focused primarily on steps taken to move forward. It appeared that a conscious effort was made to show the difference between journalism and Facebook.

The Chamber of Commerce was an unabashed cheerleader for Rockport-Fulton, as is their mission. Their consistently positive ... we will survive ... we are open for business ... communications rankled with area residents who were struggling. However, the attitude prevailed and Aransas County is surviving and is open for business, in contrast to other communities in the area.

- Want support? You will get it.
- Want sympathy? Some, tempered with "let's get on with it."
- Want to complain? "Come back next week."
- Got a crazy idea for a party? "Come on in!"

The harbor was filled with debris from sunken boats; the beach was impossible to keep clean because every tide brought in new junk; Little Bay was the recipient of massive amounts of debris from Key Allegro. There was only one place in downtown Rockport where more than 100 people could gather. That was the Woman's Club and it was filled with SBA and FEMA. Restaurants that could open had no staff because low rent housing was gone. What to do?

Of course!! We're talking about Rockport-Fulton here.

Have a party! SeaFair had a 42 year history in Rockport; it filled the quiet time between summer visitors and winter visitors. A parade ... food ... entertainment ... food ... crab races ... a gumbo cook-off ... arts and crafts market. SeaFair, in a different form would be held on October 12 thru the 15th in the outdoor gathering place ... near the harbor and the beach filled with trash. Aransas County Navigation District, on whose land SeaFair was traditionally held, firmly believed that the entire town had lost its mind. And then started to work frantically to be ready.

And yet, October was a turning point. Castaways thrift store, a community institution, reopened October 2 on a limited schedule. Government services were consolidated in an air-conditioned tent, making it more convenient to be in the wrong line. Rockport-Fulton Chamber of Commerce hosted Asleep at the Wheel on October 6 for a free concert. Teachers were back in classrooms on October 9, six weeks after Harvey, and kids back on October 11. The school's Homecoming was on October 16, a celebration of coming home for the current students and staff. The first home football game was on October 20. The first home volleyball game was on October 24.

Flood waters along Hwy 35 Business

THE KINDNESS OF STRANGERS

The wind had hardly died down and the rain stopped when a sports team from Sinton showed up in my front yard. "What are you doing here?" was my first question.

Saltwater Pavilion at Rockport Beach Park

Rockport Aquarium at Rockport Harbor

"We're here to help. What do you need?" I could hardly answer. There were so many needs. They were followed by several more groups over the first few days, all equipped to help. Some with chain saws and trucks; others with food and supplies; others with generators. I was overwhelmed.

As a Winter Texan, I felt powerless. I had limited money, limited skills, and did not want to be part of the problem by going there. So, I decided that my "mission trip" this year would be to go to Rockport and support businesses that would reopen and tip generously the persons who provided services to me. Perhaps, I could write a book ...

Volunteers were just amazing. Two different groups from Episcopal churches came and built me a 30-foot ramp to replace the one destroyed by Harvey.

I was stressed ... near the end of my rope. I was hungry and so was my husband. Despite downed power lines and debris in the road, I got into town and saw a food trailer, Mac's Pit Barbecue, serving free lunch and breakfast. He asked what he could get for me and I suggested tranquilizers. He smiled and said that he had already put them in my sandwich. He was from Brady, Texas, a long way from here, and he stayed for two weeks.

Our friend from Alaska had been building a trailer that would serve as a mobile shop for work he was doing in Alaska. After he talked with my husband about Harvey and Rockport, he bought a used camper shell for his pickup and loaded up his trailer and headed south ... with a buddy ... in December ... 5 hours of daylight a day ... in ice and snow...sleeping with no heat in his camper shell. He arrived after Christmas and is planning to stay

Not Gone With The Wind

through the end of January. He has been working on repair projects, especially for churches.

I am impressed by the army of dedicated workers rebuilding all over town, especially the roofers. We watch them way up high, some days in freezing cold and drizzling rain, working till well past sunset including on

Rockport Rotary Club helped distribute supplies flown in from Hawaii.

Saturdays and Sundays. The sea of blue tarps covering roofs all over the area is gradually diminishing.

Men from our Blue Lagoons RV Park have rebuilt the pier, constructed ramps, and are working on the fence. Residents are regularly cooking outside to feed others residents in the park who need food and taking food to feed 30 people at an Aransas Pass motel.

I am a resident of Rockport and a volunteer at the Rockport Aquarium. It took several days before I could finally get through the debris to get to the Aquarium and see that it was flattened. I was devastated. We crawled in through the destruction and began to get out the native species ... sort of a bucket brigade. One person at the tank passed the fish to the next person in line until we finally released them all into the bay. The non-native, invasive species, sadly, committed suicide in their tanks. Marley, our eel, we had gotten to the Corpus Christi Aquarium before the storm. It amazed me the number of people who wanted to know if Marley survived. But my aquarium was gone.

Our RV park has a Winter Texan fan club and a Summer Fishing fan club. As a rule, Winter Texans are older and not inclined to tackle large trees with chain saws. However, shortly after Harvey left, the summer folk, mostly younger, began arriving ... complete with chain saws and other handy tools. They began the work of rebuilding the park. We fed them.

We evacuated, first to Fredricksburg, then to New Braunfels. Since we were only going to be gone a day or so, we had done no particular preparation ... 2 days of clothes was all we had. Big mistake!! We ended up being gone for 23 days. Thank goodness for credit cards. We stayed in a small motel for two weeks and were amazed when the first home-cooked meals started showing up. We were fed for two weeks by local folk and the Salvation Army. Food and the feeling of being cared for is an enormous comfort when you are displaced.

We had no power in the church so no air conditioning. Help came from an unexpected source. When the Vice-president Pence came to visit the church and volunteer center, a member of his entourage set up our generator so we could run an ice machine. What a gift!

My father, a World War II veteran, was always helping

someone. I grew up with him as a role model. I also take the Bible seriously when we are told to help our neighbor. We had moved to Rockport from Arizona and I still missed the dry heat. But I was in the right place at the right time. There were unlimited opportunities to help and that is just what I do. I am also sustained by the number of kindred souls that I have met as they came to help.

I am amazed, as a volunteer coordinator for Volunteer Resource Center, at the long term dedication to Rockport shown by some groups. For example, the Texas Baptist Men have donated over 28,000 volunteer hours as of January 25, 2018. They have fed all the volunteers, worked for months at demolition and site cleanup, and cleaned out damaged homes. They are now shifting to rebuilding homes. The Amish and Mennonite teams have been here for months and intend to be here for at least two years.

My friend in Corpus Christi housed me in her guest room for two weeks, complete with all the care and cosseting she could force me to take. Then she made arrangements for me to rent an empty unit two floors up from her. I am still there, almost six months later, still recipient of chicken soup and a standing invitation to drinks at 5:00. My house? The contractor says he will be there tomorrow. Where would I be without the kindness of friends.

In a disaster, your friends are your wealth. Friends from Bastrop in AWD vehicles came to evacuate the animals; friends donated supplies; friends provided emergency care for the dogs; friends brought us people food and supplies. I don't think we went to a store for 6 weeks. I was so grateful because we didn't have time for anything but walking dogs and surviving.

Like any hysterical hurricane survivor, I called my contractor first. He was there in 10 minutes and I turned the house over to him to get it livable. I didn't realize at the time what a blessing he was. But the yard ... the trees ... TWIA ... it was just too much.

Volunteers came from many places. This groups is from Highlands Univ.

The Rockport-Fulton Chamber of Commerce sent me a bus ticket home from Austin; the church from Iowa came in and made extensive repairs to my home. I had no connection to either one. But now I do. I understand the idea of Pay It Forward.

My granddaughter and her friends from Texas State had visited often to enjoy the fishing and the sun. As soon as phone service was available she called to check on Mimi and Papa. I said that we were fine but there was so much damage to the trees and so much debris. We'll take care of it and see you soon she said. Not many days later, two trucks full of college kids pulled in, complete with chainsaws and rakes ... followed by ten truckloads of people from their churches and they started in on the brush. They came with their own food and water ... wouldn't let us pay for anything. I don't know what we would have done without our children and the kindness of strangers. So I made a donation to our church, which was badly damaged, in the name of those church volunteers.

All those trees down, huge live oaks, brush unending... it looked impossible for my son to clear a path to the houses alone. Then toward the end of the first week, a group of 20 folks from Ft. Worth, complete with three big Bobcats, showed up and started in. They worked for one whole day, refused any payment, and wouldn't even let us feed them. A week later, another group of five with Bobcats came to work. The driveway was usable. We felt hope again. The rest of the downed trees would just have to wait.

Orange-shirted volunteers are from Samaritian's Purse.

The Aftermath: Power

Volunteers and their help range from crucial to chaotic; sometimes both at the same time. A volunteer system usually forms in response to both the crucial needs for their help and the chaos that generates the need. The system has delegators and doers. One without the other is chaos of another form. Delegators sit in one spot where people can find them, making them a target of sorts. Their phone rings constantly, email and text messages pile up, and a line forms in front of them, wherever they are. They most often are heard saying "We can help you with that." Doers, on the other hand, have to see progress. Give them a chain saw and a bobcat and they are happy. They most often are heard saying, "Just give me the address and tell me what you need done." Neither delegators or doers appear to remember that weekends are a time to rest and regroup. The best systems are a beautiful sight and generally work independently of government agencies.

Harvey had barely cleared Rockport and headed to Houston before volunteers began pouring into Rockport from all over. Some individuals just loaded up their trucks, their generators, and their chainsaws and headed out to help out wherever they could. Other groups came prepared to work hard for a weekend; others now have been here for six months. Some groups were experienced in disaster relief; others had youth and energy. Many had ties to Rockport but couldn't do anything about their own situation so they helped others. All contributed. Initially, coordination was difficult since there was no central spot for volunteers to get job assignments. Gradually, existing institutions, usually churches, began to provide volunteer coordination and donation direction. A large volunteer network grew and they specialized in saying ... "We Can Work It Out."

Not Gone With The Wind

The First Baptist Church became the Volunteer Resource Center, despite the damage to their own facility. Initially, volunteers had been running a drive-through, dispensing food, toiletries, and cleaning supplies to 300 to 400 people a day, in the parking lot. By October, Hands of Hope moved to the church and expanded their operation. They began distributing donated building supplies to those who needed help. They fed and housed volunteer groups. They became the home base for Samaritan's Purse and the Texas Baptist Men's group as well as many other groups that sent mission project teams to Rockport. They worked out food and housing for the volunteers as well as sorting out tasks. Other churches did similar tasks ... these were the pros. They knew how mission work functioned. Their work was crucial.

KFC / Taco Bell in Rockport

INDEPENDENCE

Texans whose families go back many generations share several experiences. Looking at family photos of great and great-great grandparents, they often notice how old the women look. Many, when telling family stories, will say that they never saw grandpa smile. Survival is serious business. I think that children in the future may make similar observations about their grandparents who stayed in Rockport during Harvey.

Volunteer coordinators had a problem; people would call in for help and immediately call back saying that there must be others who needed help more. They could handle their problem. Texans have independence in their genes. This was a survival skill for the original settlers who had to contend with unpredictable but usually bad weather, brush determined to prevent settlement, hostile native snakes, and periodic disasters. So, when volunteers began pouring into the Rockport-Fulton area, an interesting situation began to develop. Residents wanted to be self-sufficient, even if that was not possible given the scope of the disaster. Volunteers wanted to help, particularly in situations where help was obviously needed. The woman in the wheelchair surrounded by debris said that her son would be there next weekend from Dallas and he would help her. Thank you for the offer. Residents had to learn to accept help; volunteers had to learn to respect their independence; coordinators had to learn to tell their callers that someone was already heading their way and couldn't be cancelled. A learning experience for all involved.

Then there was the woman in our park living in an old RV with her dogs and birds. She couldn't evacuate because she had no one to call and nowhere to go and no way to get there without a car. She stayed in her RV for the first part of the storm certain that it would be torn

Assistance came in all forms.

apart and then, during the eye, moved to a building in the park that looked like it would be safer. Afterwards, when I said that I would have come to get her if she called when the evacuation was announced, she said that she didn't want to be a bother. I wonder how many of the residents that did not evacuate felt that same way.

And finally, there was the guilt. Guilt for accepting help, guilt for having a house that survived with minimal damage, guilt for depending on someone else for food and water and ice, guilt for evacuating. For many, when asked for their hurricane story, the answer was that they didn't have a hurricane story. If their story did not have an unhappy ending, they thought it was not a story. Usually it didn't take more than two hours to tell that story ...

Texans, in general, value independence, whether it be personal or as part of a group. If Texans have a group of cardinal virtues, independence would be high on the list. It may be inherited from their pioneer foremothers and forefathers. Stories abound of settlers coming to Texas, under whoever currently claimed it, putting up a shelter far from other settlers and making do. Often the man of the house went off to earn money and the woman stayed in the shelter for extended periods with the kids and animals. She defended the home, children, possessions from weather, marauders and indigenous Texas wild life, successfully and unsuccessfully. The strong and lucky survived. The weak or unlucky died. Either way, independence was a necessity because there was no one else to depend on.

A disaster like Hurricane Harvey stresses the fabric of independence that Texans value. Initial statements at the state level about Texas size disasters and Texas size solutions proved to be difficult to implement. A bit like the toddler convinced that he can fix dinner but doesn't know how to turn on the water. The federal money represented by various agencies like FEMA was needed in a Texas sized disaster. Backtracking took place; time elapsed while agencies coordinated efforts. Citizens complained about delays in promised help. Independence was very difficult to maintain as a primary virtue when it was obvious that solutions needed group effort and money. Generally, individuals don't build power grids or haul millions of cubic yards of live oak debris. Individuals do provide aid in recovery by cutting brush, fixing meals, tearing out old sheetrock, rebuilding ramps for handicapped access and providing a ready shoulder to cry on. Individuals are less restricted in helping out individuals since they don't have strict guidelines for their activities if no money is involved. So, the power of the individual joined independence in the Texas group of cardinal virtues.

Home in South Rockport - some parts left untouched!

ANIMALS

My home is Rockport although I am a transplant from another part of Texas. My horse, Bunny, and I retired here. The storm developed so rapidly that I couldn't get Bunny evacuated. When I could get out the next day, Bunny's barn was blown down. No Bunny. Two days later, I went to check on her and I could see her out in the pasture but couldn't get to her. Two days more, and I could feed her carrots but grain was gone. Too much metal for her to be safe so I called my son to come help me move her. When he arrived, I couldn't find her anywhere. We searched, asked questions, no Bunny.

I knew we needed to evacuate and we had a place to go. My son's house was out of the danger zone. But my

Key Allegro Marina left in shambles.

orange cat, Punkin, was not going to travel well or stay in a strange place. He was an outdoor cat. So we had to leave him. Evidently, he and a neighbor cat stayed under a house until we returned. But every little noise made him skittish. I told him that I understood completely.

I tried to make arrangements for my three cats but at the last minute the neighbors were leaving too. So the two outside cats were on their own. I left a bag of food in a safe place surrounded by a pile of garbage cans all held in place by a U-shaped wooden structure that was once a work bench - about 6 ft wide and with 6 ft sides. It turned out to be a safe place and nothing moved. Coming back the first time I saw little damage and got some belongings and cleaned out the fridge, something I hadn't done before I left. I saw the yellow cat and told my cat sitter who had come back and she arranged to put out food.

The third cat I arranged for my cat sitter to take, since my son-in-law doesn't allow cats. Then she had to evacuate so the cat went with her to San Antonio. The cat that evacuated ended up at my granddaughter's so the cat sitter didn't have to bring him back—a well-traveled cat!

I left again, presumed on relatives in Austin, then went to Dallas and left on a two-week trip with my brother and sister-in-law. Finally coming home I found that power and clean water had been restored. I arranged for minor repairs and felt blessed to have survived with so few problems.

And the other outside cat showed up!

Then there is the lonely little black lab we frequently see trotting determinedly along Fulton Beach Road. He is on a mission, maybe in search of food, maybe trying to find his owners. One lady has been trying to coax him with food and would adopt him if he would let her near. I hope she succeeds. One wonders how many other pets have become lost or had to be abandoned.

Mom and Dad ran away from home on Friday morning, leaving us eleven kids and five worthless cats behind. We had no shelter so we mostly hung out on the patio. Fortunately, they had the sense to take the dog. Talk about a worthless animal! And they stayed away for weeks. At least when they came back, they noticed that neighborhood dogs were chasing us and got us our own donkey. That donkey is wicked!!! More help than mom and dad were, that's for sure. But we goats were survivors. Not going to let a little thing like a Category 4 hurricane get us!

We have no idea what happened but when we got back from New Mexico, we checked our fish pond. It was

Aerial view of Key Allegro after Harvey.

surrounded by big catfish carcasses. How did they get out? Storm surge washed them out? Wind blew them out? Harvey sucked them out? If catfish can be spoiled pets, these were. Fed twice a day, they recognized my wife, the catfish whisperer. I guess we'll just have to restock the pond,

We have lived in Rockport for 5 generations. On Friday, August 25, we loaded up to evacuate. Six adults, 7 children, 1 German Shepherd, 1 cat, 1 English Collie and 1 Border Collie. All loaded up but suddenly, no cat. Rosie, Kathleen's cat, was nowhere to be found. We unloaded and looked ... no Rosie ... so we had to leave without her. We said prayers for her safety and left. Two weeks later, I was home doing laundry and heard a weak "Meow!" Sure enough, it was Rosie, very weak, battered, ears mangled; Rosie was home.

Ready for dip in the pool at a condo complex on Key Allegro.

We have always had a lab. Gem, our last lab, died in July, 2017. We weren't ready for another dog and had given all of Gem's stuff away. Then came Harvey; lots of animals needed homes. And with Harvey came Chester. Chester needed a home and we figured we needed a dog. A perfect fit. He likes his new bed and he loves us. We still have always had a lab.

A tossed RV

We evacuated my horse, Skippa Dandy "Dan", to Fredricksburg and it was a good thing. His barn here was destroyed in the hurricane. He stayed there to be safe but after three weeks, he developed a case of severe colic and passed away. He was my soul mate ... truly God's gift to me. It won't be the same without him. I still think of him as a victim of the hurricane.

Our air-conditioner shorted out during the extreme heat after Harvey . It had been running fine so we called our service man. After a close ... then far away examination, he said that the fire ants had gotten in and shorted out all the contacts.

My horse, Bunny, had disappeared from her pasture. My son's wife, a veterinarian, posted her picture on social media and within a day, Bunny was found. Mike Valdez from Sinton had been called to pick up some horses from

Rockport and picked up Bunny also. He took her to the Stockyards in Alice, 100 miles away. He had posted the info on Facebook but we had no power so didn't see it. Thanks to social media, Bunny was found, loaded up into my son's trailer and taken to her new home.

I worried. The housing situation for people in Rockport was dire. Not much I could do. But the housing situation for herons was also dire. The blue herons had always built their nests in the tops of live oak trees, sprangly things, in groups called heronries. They come back year after year. Not only were many of the trees gone but the twigs that herons use to build the nests were still attached to the branches buried in the debris. I got birder friends together and we gathered twigs and left them in the area where the herons nested. It's hard to tell if a heron is appreciative.

As in other hurricanes, animals determined behavior. People stayed because they couldn't transport their cats; people evacuated because they didn't want their pets to be hurt. People evacuated and left animals with neighbors who were not leaving. People left their animals to fend for themselves. Outside rescue agencies came in before the storm and evacuated any animals that seemed abandoned. Snakes, with no intention of leaving St. Joe's Island, were forcibly evacuated by the wind and landed in Rockport. Cattle died.

THE AFTERMATH: THE NEW NORMAL

October 12-December 10, 2017

Aransas County

Teachers could get back in classrooms on October 9. Not "their" classrooms in most cases, but what would become their classrooms when their students came back. Schools opened to students October 11. Homecoming had new significance this year. On October 16, we celebrated a true homecoming for staff and students. Life was coming back to normal ... for students, staff, and for administrators. I began to relax. Finally, questions that I could answer.

Allergies are wicked this year. I finally realized that, in addition to the usual pollen coming from all over, mold was floating every time an old roof was demolished. And there are many old roofs and buildings being demolished or rebuilt. I think I will buy stock in Kleenex.

I haven't forgotten the shock of the "real-life" destruction we saw when we arrived here in December. We had seen photos, but were not prepared for the massive destruction of so many homes and buildings, or for the stunning piles of debris in the highway median which, we are told, are only a fraction of what was.

National Guard distributing water and ice.

The innumerable fishing piers, symbols of Rockport-Fulton's main industry and tourist attraction, are now reduced to a mass of higgledy piggledy sticks protruding from the water.

Finally, we have been impressed and touched by the tears in the eyes of many who have told us their hurricane experiences and by their spirit and determination. Not one has expressed self-pity or complained. Quite the opposite; all have felt lucky that their fate could have been so much worse. But there is no doubt that all have been traumatized to some extent by the disaster and our hearts go out to all our Texas friends who have welcomed us so warmly. Rockport-Fulton is still a beautiful town and it will recover!

The incinerators are near my home and I complain sometimes because I think that I can smell the smoke. Then the burn ban was lifted. I had no idea how much smoke could be given off by a brush pile. No further complaints about the incinerators.

I live in Aransas Pass now. My son was a senior at Rockport-Fulton High School. When we evacuated, he ended up enrolled in Portland; when Rockport schools reopened, he transferred back; shortly after, he transferred to Aransas Pass high school and will graduate from there. Harvey was emotionally difficult for high school students, especially seniors. It is hard to think about the future when the present keeps demanding your attention.

In late November, we arrived at our park where we usually stay in our motor home. Where were the birds? There are always birds ... grackles and sea gulls at least. No birds ... no bird sounds. I was amazed. Where did they go? Later, as we drove around we began to see egrets and pelicans ... and an emu and a donkey.

We are back in our park but we see the toll that Harvey took. Our potluck suppers that usually had 80 to 90 participants now have 35 to 40. About half of the sites are unoccupied. We lost over 300 big trees that gave the park its name. In some cases, units were destroyed; in others, people just decided to avoid the sight of the destruction. Some people felt they were too old to start over. Despite their affection for Rockport, the thought of looking at their beautiful town in shambles was just too much. They didn't come back.

Not Gone With The Wind

Harvey should not be seen in the past tense; I will still be dealing with residuals of Harvey for a long time. Harvey is definitely in the present tense all the time. Right now, all I want is my home back ... in Rockport ... and my mobility manageable. Check back this time next year.

Workmen, whose work we inspected at a neighbor's project, are in the house. Or not in the house much. They arrive at 11, take a lunch break, work for a couple of hours with three smoke breaks, and leave for the day ... leaving clutter behind them. One of them had nicked the water line and it dripped ... into a pile of dirt ... at the foot of the stairs. Sure enough, I stepped in it, slipped and fell, and broke my arm. We were all at fault but I wasn't being paid to do a job. In the end, neither were they.

We celebrated Thanksgiving in my reconstructed house with all the family. My father, my granddaughter and her husband. It was a lovely occasion. The next day when I called my dad he didn't answer. When we went to check, I found him. The doctors said he had a major brain bleed, a heart attack and a stroke with no idea about the order of the events. I think the stress of the destruction was too much for him; he was a victim of Harvey.

Would I go back to Oklahoma? I think most of us know that another hurricane will come. But I still wouldn't leave. No place is perfect. This is home.

The schools are open with fewer students and teachers. Out of 1300 businesses before Harvey, about 300 have reopened. The first pass through to pick up debris is nearly finished. Mount TxDOT stretches for more than a mile along the Hwy 35 Bypass. Residents are filing damage claims with insurors, FEMA and others. SBA is making loans.

Winter Texans who have a place to stay are coming to town. RV parks have made huge efforts to have places for their usual visitors. Residents are used to Rockport being beautiful; Rockport is not beautiful now. Signs of depression abound. SeaFair in October had provided a break but many residents feel that Harvey is still here, grinding away, without an end in sight. What to do... of course, another party. Tropical Christmas can't be cancelled. ACND is still certain that the town is delusional but gets ready for another party.

The first home football game was on October 20.

Trees damaged at Goose Island State Park.

The volleyball team's gym was destroyed so they played almost their entire season on the road; their first home volleyball game was on October 24. A touch of normal for a shattered town.

*Within eight weeks -
leaves were returning to the trees.*

HARVEY'S TOLL AS OF DECEMBER, 2017:

Year Round Population of Aransas County, including Rockport-Fulton-Lamar: at least 25% of the population has not returned, primarily because of lack of housing

Seasonal Population including Winter Texans: 50% of Winter Texans have not returned, primarily those who rented in permanent structures like houses and condos that were heavily damaged. Many residents of trailer parks who lost their homes have not returned.

School District enrollment: 2400 25% of students have not re-enrolled. Repairs continue.

Rockport City Hall: Structure was heavily damaged.

Aransas County Courthouse: Structure was heavily damaged and will be demolished.

Fulton Convention Center (Paws and Taws): Structure was heavily damaged and will be demolished.

Major Attractions:
- Extensive facilities for hiking, biking and kayaking: Debris has been removed and many are now open.
- Excellent fishing: Fishing is recovering.
- Excellent birding: Migrating birds and native populations have been disrupted and are recovering. Hummingbirds didn't get the memo and came anyway. Volunteers brought in feeders but population is still down.

Services:
- Churches: Rebuilding and missions continue
- Campgrounds and RV parks: Many have reopened with limitations; no swimming pools and community

rooms; damaged piers. Rebuilding continues.

- Condominium developments: The least damaged developments have reopened, mostly to their permanent residents. Rental units are limited.
- Bait shops: Those in the harbors are mostly demolished and will be rebuilt.
- Beach structures: None are usable; the only survivor is the small structure. All are being rebuilt.
- Fishing guides: Fishing appears to be improving.
- General contractors: They have difficulty getting enough skilled workers but are making progress.
- Hotels and motels: La Quinta, of the larger hotels, opened fairly early. Several are advertising for staff. Most have not reopened but are rebuilding.
- Restaurants: After rebuilding, restaurants are having difficulty finding staff. Housing shortage continues to be an issue.
- Volunteer Fire Departments, Police and Sheriff departments: Equipment is being replaced but limited housing impacts staffing.

TREES

I am a Rockport resident. I went out on my front porch after it appeared the hurricane was over and burst into tears. The line of 100-year-old oaks in my front yard were gone; there were no leaves left on any other trees. Though damage was limited in the house, my trees were gone. I was devastated.

I believe that my house was built around a tree limb ... not the whole tree ... but the limb. It leans across the front of the house and is propped up by a pillar that is slowly being absorbed by the limb. After Harvey, neighbors came by to see if the limb survived ... and secondarily, to see if the house had survived if the limb had not. It had survived as did the house. My son evaluated the limb and decided a bit of reinforcement would not be amiss and put in another prop. Should be good until the next Category 5 hurricane.

I found it fascinating from the Mayor's letters that, by August 30, Texas A&M Forestry Service was developing

Sprawling Live Oaks in front of HEB.

Not Gone With The Wind

materials for homeowners about whether a tree could be saved. A team would eventually evaluate most of the trees in the urban areas and make recommendations about portions of the tree to remove, to keep, and how to go about saving the trees. In the rush to reestablish roads and access to houses, it appears that many trees were damaged unnecessarily and would probably die. Who knew that trimming up the broken stubs was the wrong thing to do? Foresters were as stressed as the trees that they were protecting.

The leaves were all gone ... just gone. The tree branches were shades of grey, all their twistedness exposed without leaves. Houses that had been hidden in the middle of 5 acres were suddenly visible. Neighbors could see houses that they hadn't noticed in years. The damage to Rockport was starkly obvious. People cried because of what they now could see so clearly. All the trees looked dead.

Not only could we see nearby neighbors; we could also see neighbors farther away. With no trees, we could tell when someone needed help with a project and headed on over. We discovered that we enjoyed the company of the neighborhood and vowed to get together more often.

I lost four big live oaks, one over two hundred years old. Houses can be rebuilt; live oaks, not so much. I still mourn that tree. It had shaded my entire back yard.

Friends on Goose Island near the Big Tree had just had their trees' ages determined during the summer of 2017. One was 500 years old in their backyard. Harvey got it. Houses can be rebuilt. But a 500 year old tree ... priceless.

I am still on YouTube, searching for places I recognized.

Somewhere I heard that the Big Tree was OK. I think I would have been crushed if Big Tree had been destroyed. 1000 years, probably 20 hurricanes ... it was a symbol of resilience to me. Odd how I would have mourned a tree.

Rockport is an artist colony, well known for beautiful water vistas, birds, flowers and palm trees. But what did residents mourn after coming back from evacuation? Their trees ... not the tall graceful palms but their iconic live oak trees. Live oaks are not towering ... are not graceful, particularly as they age. They may look like they have warts, are twisted and often depend on crutches to hold their limbs off the ground. If a tree could use a walker, the live oak would be the first candidate to give it a try. They shed leaves but are rarely without leaves at all. But an old live oak has dignity ... it may never, in its long life, have been naked. After Harvey, there were no leaves. Think of a Baptist suddenly transported to a nudist colony.

The live oaks demand pride of place; they are trees with attitude. Many houses in old Rockport have obviously been built around the tree. The old roads are routed around the trees with no attention paid to north and south. No need for speed limit signs. Too much speed and your car's paint job will join the numerous shades of paint on the tree trunk. Live oaks don't tower ... they spread and loom.

Tourists going to see The Big Tree may think that they will see a Sequoia as it is probably the oldest tree in Texas at 1000 years old. Nope ... think crotchety old grandfather of a tree ... seen it all and is not impressed. It was the live oaks that contributed to 3.1 million cubic yards of debris in a county of 25,000 people. Massive trees, hundreds of years old, were uprooted or broken off and often deposited by the wind in the least convenient place, like the middle of the house or highway. They did not go quietly ... when they went, they took anything in the area along with them. No ballet performance with graceful kneeling; more like the mayhem of a hard-fought touchdown. No victory dance for the live oaks though. Undignified.

In the open areas in Aransas County, live oaks create colonies around the main tree, spreading from their roots with the enthusiastic cooperation of local wildlife. The resulting underbrush is almost impenetrable. People in Rockport don't have live oaks as specimen trees very often; they have living brush piles. Transplanted Texans from colder climates may be used to grooming their landscaping, leaving tidy vistas They either give it up as a bad job in a tropical climate or invest in a Bobcat and a sturdy chainsaw.

Yet, seeing thousands of hundred year old trees destroyed by Harvey affected residents profoundly. Oh, and the Big Tree? Survived a direct hit by a Category 4 hurricane. It was probably at least the 20th hurricane to go through during the 1000 years it has been there.

Home along Little Bay in Rockport

THE AFTERMATH: THE NEW NORMAL

In Conclusion

I am amazed. Some of our big oaks just broke off mid-trunk. We hauled off the ones that were uprooted and figured we would deal with the broken ones later. I looked out the other day and there were small sprigs growing out of those broken trees. They were survivors. We'll leave them alone and give them a chance. I think that Rockport is like those stumps ... surviving and sending out new shoots.

Uprooted Live Oak Tree in Lamar

Not Gone With The Wind

Condos in Rockport

Boat Barn at Cove Harbor

ACKNOWLEDGMENTS

Thank you to all the contributors to the stories:

Tomme Actkinson, Rockport resident

Shirley Barrett, Rockport resident

Dodi Dix, Rockport resident

Modena Durkee, Rockport transplant

Melody Field, Rockport resident

Tom Garrett, Winter Texan from Oklahoma

Jody Gilbert, Rockport transplant

Carita Gould, Rockport resident

Don/Sara Hander, Rockport residents

Joyce Harmsen, Winter Texan from Wyoming

Annette Hegen, Rockport resident

Mary Kay Herrington, Rockport resident

Jean Holland, Rockport transplant

Irene Holmes, Winter Texan from Ontario

Hoppy/Sandy Hopkins, Winter Texans from Canada

Rosemary Kelley, Refugio resident

Sam Kenny, Rockport resident

Barbara Lavely, Rockport transplant from Michigan

Liska Malcolm, Rockport resident

Mary Anne McBride, Rockport resident

Liz McDuff, Rockport resident

Rick McLester, Emergency Operations Coordinator,

Fulton Police Chief, Fire Chief and probably the town plumber

Dana Mercer, Rockport resident, veterinarian

Jennifer Mullins, Rockport resident

Helen Nerod, Rockport resident

Debbie Oliver, Rockport resident

Mathew Otero, Rockport resident

Joey Patek, Rockport resident, Superintendent, ACISD

Nancy Paulson, Rockport resident

Cyndi Powell, Rockport resident

Russ/Kathe Powers, Rockport residents

James/Glynn Reed, Rockport residents

Charles Reed, Rockport resident

Suzanne Reuber, Winter Texan from Kansas

Pat Rios, Rockport resident, Mayor Pro Tem of Rockport

Iris Sanchez, Rockport resident, librarian

Gina Satterbo, Rockport resident

Cecelia Seibert, Rockport resident

Kathleen Shaftic, Winter Texan from Montana

Nina Shannon, Rockport resident

Frank/Dotty Shaughnessy, Rockport residents

Elaine Shoemaker, Winter Texan

Tricia Siler, Rockport resident

Kathy Steele, Winter Texan from Iowa

Sally Sughroue, Winter Texan from Nebraska

Ruthalea Taylor, Rockport resident

Elaine Timmins, Rockport resident

Peggy Wanderscheid, Rockport resident

CJ Wax, Rockport resident, Mayor of Rockport

Mitchel Wess, Rockport transplant

Carolyn Whitener, Winter Texan

Karolann Whitsell, Winter Texan

Liska Malcolm, Rockport resident

William/Alex , Rockport residents

All the others who generously told me stories

Thank you to Volunteer Organizations

Mercy Chefs (faith based, non-profit disaster relief organization): thank you for serving professionally prepared meals to victims, volunteers and first responders after Harvey

Loads of Hope (one branch of Matthew 25 Ministries, an international humanitarian aid and disaster relief organization): thanks for providing clean clothes

Red Cross: thank you for assistance with shelter, food, clothing and other emergency needs

Coastal Oaks Baptist Church and all the other churches: thanks for providing a donation and distribution point for donations

Operation Blessing: thanks for yard cleanup

Texas A&M Veterinarian Emergency Team: thanks for providing emergency services to pets

Detroit Police Department: thanks for the truckload of goods for law enforcement personnel

Samaritan's Purse: thank you for cleaning up, tearing down, and rebuilding

Not Gone With The Wind

UMCOR: thanks for disaster recovery help

Texas Baptist Men: thanks for feeding volunteers and providing disaster recovery services

Mennonites: thanks for the help in rebuilding

Amish: thanks for the help in rebuilding

First Baptist Church: thanks for providing space for a Volunteer Resource Center and for numerous mission groups coming in to help in Aransas County

Castaways: thanks for your continuing mission

CSDR (Church of Scientology Disaster Response Organization): thanks for all the building materials

High School students from St. Patrick Academy, Providence, Rhode Island: thanks for helping to clear debris

Heartfelt thanks to the thousands of individuals who have come to help Rockport rebuild, both as part of groups and as individuals who said that they just couldn't stay away

Thank you to Government and 501c3 Organizations

ACISD (Aransas County Independent School District): thanks for providing educational services for students in Aransas County

ACND (Aransas County Navigation District): thanks for cleanup and restoration of numerous properties on the waterfront in Rockport, Fulton, Lamar and Aransas County.

Aransas County Government: thanks for providing leadership during and after Hurricane Harvey

Acknowledgments

BOAT (Building Officials Association of Texas): thanks for evaluating all facilities in Arransas County to determine livability and continuing operation

CBDRG (Coastal Bend Disaster Recovery Group): thanks for your coordination services

FEMA (Federal Emergency Management Agency): thanks for providing assistance after Harvey

Federal HUD (Housing and Urban Development): thanks for administering Community Development Block Grant Program

Fulton, TX Town Government: thanks for providing leadership during and after Hurricane Harvey

Public Works: thanks for working to restore utilities

Parks: thanks for working to get parks ready for residents

Police and Public Safety: thanks for keeping us safe

Rockport-Fulton Chamber of Commerce: thanks for supporting the rebuilding of Rockport

Rockport, TX City Government: thanks for providing leadership during and after Hurricane Harvey

SBA (Small Business Administration): thanks for making loans to help businesses and homeowners to repair or replace damaged or destroyed real estate

TCEQ (Texas Commission on Environmental Quality): thanks for your work on disposing of debris

TDH (Texas Department of Health): thanks for free tetanus shots

TDI (Texas Department of Insurance): thanks for answering questions about insurance

TEA (Texas Education Agency): thanks for coordinating

Not Gone With The Wind

education services

TxDOT (Texas Department of Transportation): thanks for removing massive amounts of debris from roadways and creating Mount TxDOT

Texas A&M Forest Service and their Urban Forest Strike Teams: thank you for looking after our trees

TWC (Texas Workforce Commission): thanks for creating temporary jobs to aid in rebuilding after Harvey

TWIA (Texas Wind Insurance Association): thanks for providing wind and hail coverage when private insurance companies exclude coverage from homeowners and other property owners in coastal areas

Texas GLO (General Land Office): thanks for overseeing short- and long-term housing for Texans displaced by Hurricane Harvey.

UIL (University Interscholastic League): thanks for finding ways to meet the needs of students while coordinating sports programs for the state of Texas

US Coast Guard: thank you for help clearing boats out of our harbors

Woman's Club of Aransas County: thank you for space for SBA, FEMA, community meetings, and for the normalcy of gathering with friends to play games

Thank you to businesses:

AEP Texas: thanks for restoring power to Aransas Pass, Rockport, Victoria and Port Lavaca/Refugio areas so quickly

NSR (North Star Recovery): thanks for rebuilding our

schools

CCCP (Corpus Christi Cycle Plaza): thanks for the Kawasaki Mule, an all-terrain vehicle similar to its namesake, for the Aransas County Sheriff's Office

SAS (San Antonio Shoes): thanks for the shoes and socks

HEB: thanks for reopening so soon and for having gas for our generators

ACE Hardware: thanks for having what we needed

Rockport Donuts: thanks for the kolaches

Rockport Pilot: thanks for the news about Rockport-Fulton-Aransas County

Restaurants who found ways to reopen despite damage: so that workers who came to help could eat

Contractors: thanks for your help rebuilding Aransas County

Most of all, thank you to the residents who have survived, struggled, and moved ahead in rebuilding their homes and their lives.

Made in the USA
Columbia, SC
10 August 2018